Getting Boys Up and Running in the Early Years

G000245063

'A wonderfully clear and useful book, so lively and engaging, so immediately applicable to every aspect of early childhood learning. Rigorous, warm hearted and practical, a rare achievement.'

—Steve Biddulph AM, psychologist and author of *Raising Boys*

'Deeply rooted in a beautiful range of accessible observations, Julie Cigman's new book is most timely. She understands the ways boys learn and their need for risk-taking, exploration, physicality, sound role-models and expectations. The strengths of boys' play and learning are clearly valued and celebrated as is the crucial importance of creating irresistible spaces for play and learning for both boys and girls.'

—Kathryn Solly, Early Years speaker, consultant, trainer and author

A thorough, reflective and insightful analysis of how to nurture the holistic development of children, especially boys, in the Early Years. It's a must read for anyone striving to create a positive, challenging, and stimulating environment for the promotion of quality learning. A fantastic book.

—Ed Harding, Forest School Manager, Free Rangers Nursery, Bath.

Getting Boys Up and Running in the Early Years addresses the fact that boys do less well than girls in all areas of learning in the Early Years and continue to lag behind girls in assessments throughout their school careers. This book draws on current research to provide practical advice on ways in which Early Years practitioners can create positive learning environments for all children. It explores how best to match provision to all children's learning styles, aiding their progress in personal, social and emotional development, communication and language, and physical development. Final chapters show how learning in all other curriculum areas can follow, in a carefully designed environment.

Key points explored include:

- the environment we can create to enable both boys and girls to become confident and autonomous learners
- ways that practitioners can evaluate and enhance provision to improve levels of well-being and involvement
- physical development and the value of active, challenging and adventurous play
- practical ways to stimulate language development
- planned activities and rich experiences that support holistic learning in an inspiring environment.

Giving clear guidance on helping boys to meet high expectations in a playful and creative way, *Getting Boys Up and Running in the Early Years* is an essential read for anyone working to create a positive foundation for boys in Early Years education.

Julie Cigman is an Early Years teacher, trainer and consultant. She runs projects, courses and workshops on early writing and supporting boys' learning in the EYFS. She is author of *Supporting Boys' Writing in the Early Years: Becoming a writer in leaps and bounds.*

Getting Boys Up and Running in the Early Years

Creating stimulating places and spaces for learning

Julie Cigman

Routledge
Taylor & Francis Group

LONDON AND NEW YORK

First published 2017
by Routledge
2 Park Square, Milton Park, Abingdon, Oxon OX14 4RN

and by Routledge
711 Third Avenue, New York, NY 10017

Routledge is an imprint of the Taylor & Francis Group, an informa business

British Library Cataloguing in Publication Data
A catalogue record for this book is available from the British Library

Library of Congress Cataloging in Publication Data
A catalog record for this book has been requested

ISBN: 978-1-138-86001-8 (hbk)
ISBN: 978-1-138-86002-5 (pbk)
ISBN: 978-1-315-71682-4 (ebk)

Typeset in Optima
by Swales & Willis Ltd, Exeter, Devon, UK

To my grandchildren, who get me up and running!

Contents

Acknowledgements   xi
Foreword   xiii

Introduction   1

Background   1
Who is this book for?   2
A vision of childhood   2
Social constructivism   3
What is this book about?   5

1 Creating an enabling learning environment for boys and girls   7

Introduction   7
What do we know about how all children learn?   7

2 Pink, blue or purple: gender identity and early learning   17

Introduction   17
1 Male and female differences: biology or environmental
   influences?   18
2 How can we mitigate any limiting impact of biological and
   environmental influences on gender identity?   22
3 Practical ways to challenge gender stereotypes with young
   children   25

3 Pushing back the boundaries for learning   31

Introduction   31
1 Creating an inclusive learning environment for boys and girls   32
2 Safety to explore and take risks   34
3 Practical ways to set appropriate boundaries and expectations   39

4 Creating irresistible spaces for play and learning   45

Introduction   45
1 Getting the environment right for boys – and girls   45
2 Matching provision to the learning styles and interests of boys   48
3 Lifting the lid on learning: creating a tinkering workshop   52

5 Becoming a confident mover   61

Introduction   61
1 Evaluating the environment to support boys' learning styles   62
2 Why do children need to move?   63
3 Planning the physical environment to support active learning   65
4 Resources to promote fine and gross motor skills   70
5 Some activities to encourage fine and gross motor development   73
6 Some practicalities and management issues   74
7 Sharing benefits of active play with parents (and all staff)   76

6 Becoming a confident communicator   79

Introduction   79
1 Acquiring early language skills   79
2 What shall we talk about?   82
3 Who shall we talk to? The role of the adult   84
4 Time to talk: some starting points for talking with boys   87
5 Where shall we talk? Creating language-rich spaces and places   89
6 Parents   95

7 Planning for cross-curricular learning   97

Introduction   97
1 'Whatever you want to become' learning   98
2 Planning the learning environment   100
3 Responding to children's schematic play   108
4 Involving parents   111

8 Creating spaces and places to get boys up and running   115

Introduction   115
1 Young engineers, architects and inventors   116
2 Young botanists, lepidopterists and zoologists   119
3 Young farmers and cooks   121
4 Young musicians, artists and performers   122
5 Young writers and poets   126

Conclusion   129

References and further reading   131
Index   135

Acknowledgements

This book was made possible by standing on the shoulders of giants, and some of the tallest giants have been small children. Special thanks go to my grandchildren and nephew, Arlo, Sennen, Sophia, Dylan, Charlie, Suzy and Sam, who uninhibitedly share their lives and their unique way of seeing and responding to the world. Their voices resound throughout the book. Other unique voices come from children who I have had the privilege to be alongside, in schools and Early Years settings in England, Iceland, Denmark and New Zealand.

Thanks to staff and children in Jump Primary, Wellgate Primary and Athergate North in Barnsley, Nicole Miller and her team at Rickley Park in Bletchley, Matthew Caldwell and team at Knowle West Children's Centre in Bristol, Lesley Garfoot and her team at Headington Quarry Foundation Stage School in Oxford, and staff at Reykjakot and Managardur in Iceland, who were so hospitable and generous with their time and expertise.

Thanks, too, to Tim Graham and Ed Harding, who took the time to share their expertise in outdoor learning, and to Tom Hobson, Andrew Clifford, Annette Parsons and Jess Mitchell, who shared their creative ideas and thinking.

Finally, thanks to Martin, who once again has done a phenomenal job, reading chapters as they were written and making constructive comments, and to Rachel, Amelia, Simon and Yasmin, for keeping their faith in me whenever I was in danger of losing faith in myself.

Foreword

One of the constant challenges as an Early Years educator is that of resolving the tension between external pressures to standardise the nature of children, and our own knowledge – and experience – of the infinite diversity that exists. The nature of individual children, shaped by their genes, experiences, contexts and cultures, creates the very real daily challenge of how to meet, support and extend their appropriate and meaningful learning and development. As we remain committed to the critical importance of a 'learner-centred' approach, the need to define how this relates to the specific needs of children becomes ever more salient. Equally, an approach to pedagogy that enables the flexibility to adapt provision, environments, resources and interactions has rightly become a central professional concern.

Within this diverse range of individualities lies the issue of boys' learning and development, how – and if – this is a significant aspect, whether this is innate or learned, and how this can be understood, especially within what is generally a highly feminised environment in which boys often identify themselves as 'other'. In many ways, the examination of this as a specific challenge provides the means to address a mindset and create an approach that can be truly 'learner-centred'.

Julie Cigman's highly respected and influential work exploring the issues and challenges of providing learning experiences that account for and mitigate the influence of gender identity has long been valued throughout the Early Years community.

This book provides a timely and significant dimension to the wider debate around developmentally appropriate provision and the specific issues of boys' inclusion. Research indicates that boys from particular social and cultural contexts are likely to be the most sensitive to the effects of quality in their setting. Most importantly, this can make the most significant contribution to what is often termed 'closing the gap'. Indeed, provision which meets the needs of this group often acts as a 'barometer' to the overall quality of the provision for all children.

Drawing as it does upon the most up-to-date and relevant research, this book is also deeply rooted within the fundamental principles of effective Early Years pedagogy and clearly builds on the work of early pioneers in childhood education. Central to their work was establishing the conditions – physical, emotional and cognitive – for how effective learning and development could be supported. As now, these pioneers stressed the importance of play, recognising the individual learner, the central role of children's well-being and the critical importance of the role of the adult. The latter is not just highly influential in terms of effective and sensitive interaction, but also in terms of how the ethos of that relationship is structured and, in particular, how attitudes towards gender identity are formed, supported and – where necessary – challenged.

What is also unique and remarkable about this book is that within the exploration of theory, research and philosophy lies a deeply practical and accessible set of ideas and approaches that can facilitate this. I consider it an honour to be able to introduce this text as an invaluable and essential book with which to clarify and support effective Early Years practice.

Jan Dubiel
National Director, Early Excellence

Introduction

Our task . . . is to help the children climb their own mountains, as high as possible. No one can do more.

(Loris Malaguzzi)

Background

> Declan is two and a few months. He stands in the outside area of his nursery, looking at a mini 'assault course' made from some wooden planks and pallets. Watching him, it's almost possible to see his thought bubble: *That looks fun! Can I do it? I think I'll have a go.*
>
> He steps onto a sloping plank that leads up to one of the pallets. The plank wobbles and Declan stops, steadies himself by crouching down and lowering his centre of gravity, then he carries on climbing. He jumps off the last pallet and goes round the course again with increased confidence.

'Boys' underachievement' has been a topic of concern for educators and policymakers in the UK and in countries across the world for many years. This book explores how boys' underachievement in the early years can be tackled, drawing on recent research studies and numerous observations of boys made in a wide range of settings in the UK, Denmark, New Zealand, Italy and Iceland. It challenges the use of purely academic measures of achievement and investigates how we can create an environment where children like Declan can build up their 'knowledge, values and identity' (Moss 2005: 27).

When children fail to thrive in educational settings, we need to be clear if the failure to thrive is due to a child's lack of engagement with the learning environment, rather than lack of ability. We need to evaluate the reasons for their disenchantment. In a heavily female-dominated profession, women practitioners need to be able to step into boys' shoes and see the world from their perspective. We can raise the confidence of boys as learners and also raise their attainment by respecting all styles of learning and by creating an irresistible environment that will enchant and engage them. This is possible in a fluid and flexible environment that caters for the spectrum of boys' behaviour and interests; that recognises similarities and differences in the way that boys and girls behave and learn; and that allows boys and girls to explore a range and variety of learning opportunities in a non-prescriptive environment.

A significant number of boys don't manage to 'get up and running' successfully in the early years. These boys are in danger of being branded as underachieving by the age of 5, engendering a poor sense of themselves as learners before they even start statutory schooling. However, we can get it right for the boys, and when we do, we will get it right for all children.

Who is this book for?

This book has been written to provide a source of pedagogical underpinning and practical ideas for all early years practitioners, including teachers and support staff in nursery and reception classes, Key Stage 1 teachers, staff working in day nurseries, early years leaders, children's centre leaders, head teachers and childminders. It can also provide a useful resource for teacher training providers, university and college lecturers, students, and parents of young children. It supports practitioners to articulate their vision for developmentally appropriate provision for boys and for all children so that this vision can be shared with parents, senior management and Ofsted.

A vision of childhood

> Education is not an affair of 'telling' and being told, but an active and constructive process.
>
> (Dewey 1916: 38)

Loris Malaguzzi described knowledge as being 'like "a tangle of spaghetti" with no beginning, middle or end, but always shooting off in new directions' (Moss 2005: 26). Children need to be brave and curious investigators when they encounter this 'tangle of spaghetti' and this can sometimes create mess and confusion, especially with our young boys! In this book we explore ways to create a learning environment where:

- the environment can be messy in the way that a laboratory or construction site is messy: as a space where learning is work in progress;
- children's curiosity can be directed into activities that are adventurous, but where risk is minimised;
- children can learn how to handle materials appropriately, understanding that they can throw a ball or a beanbag, but not a slice of toast or a rock; they can pour water into a water tray or puddle but not on the floor inside;
- children can move rapidly, chasing swirling leaves and racing down a slope, and they can move slowly and carefully, looking for bugs under logs or noticing the patterns on the bark of a tree.

In this way, children are beginning to learn not only the immutable laws of nature through scientific and mathematical investigation, but they are also beginning to learn social laws and customs so that they can function safely and healthily in a community.

Social constructivism

Ed and Jemma take a group of four children down to a brook, a short walk away.

- The adults agree explicit boundaries and, once these are established, they trust the children and expect the trust to be mutual. The children run ahead as far as the gate and are reminded of the rules that they have all discussed: *As far as the gate, and wait there. Thanks for waiting, guys.*
- Children are allowed the autonomy to direct their learning when possible. The outing has no predefined purpose, but the adults are aware of the rich potential learning and children can guide the direction of their experience.
- Children are expected to take responsibility for their learning at appropriate times. When Nicholas says: *I'm wet*, Ed reminds him gently that he's been running in the water. Nicholas doesn't complain, because he knows that he is responsible for his wet trousers and that there are dry clothes back at the setting.

(continued)

(continued)

- The adults make suggestions, give guidance, and support children's self-regulation and decision-making: Ed notices that Laurie is watching two children who have waded into the brook. *Do you want to go in? It's shallower up here. How high are your boots?*

- They provide information and model 'not knowing': *You've caught a water shrimp! I'm not sure what else you've got there. I'll take a picture and we can look it up when we get back.*

- Children help each other and make suggestions: two boys are climbing a tree by the brook. William tells his friend: *Here's an easier way to get down.* And he catches hold of a branch, swings and drops down.

The atmosphere is calm and orderly. The children move between active, energetic play and still and purposeful activity.

Children actively construct their learning in an environment that invites them to explore and investigate ideas, materials and ways of being. Adults actively construct their understanding of how children learn, typically and as individuals, through involvement with children in their play and explorations: stepping back, observing and reflecting, and being researchers to identify children's 'zone of proximal development' (Vygotsky 1978: 86). In this way, practitioners can facilitate children's independence wherever possible (William was very capable of getting down from the tree and Declan worked out how to find his balance on a wobbly plank) and give specific support when it is needed (guiding Laurie to take the first steps into the brook) *to do today what they will be able to do independently tomorrow* (Vygotsky 1978).

Children learn best when relationships involve mutual respect: when a dynamic is established that values the unique response of each adult and child to the world, and engenders excitement and pleasure in the process of learning and co-constructing meaning.

What is this book about?

When I first started planning this book, I envisaged that each chapter would focus on one area of the curriculum. As I started writing, it became clear that the learning environment cannot be compartmentalised into chapters any more than children's learning can be compartmentalised.

Chapter 1 focuses on the characteristics of effective young learners and asks what kind of environment we want to create to enable all children to become confident and autonomous learners.

In Chapter 2 we explore the extent to which differences between boys and girls are biologically determined. We consider how biological differences can impact on children's learning and attainment in early schooling if we allow these differences to limit our expectations of boys.

Chapter 3 investigates how we can extend the boundaries for learning to create an environment that allows young boys to have significant freedom and flexibility in the way that they learn.

In Chapter 4 we explore ways in which practitioners can evaluate and enhance their provision to improve boys' levels of well-being and involvement.

William is working hard to start a fire with a fire steel and some cotton wool. He has been shown how to hold and strike the fire steel and how to fluff up the cotton wool to help it to catch the sparks: Ed, I did it! Is it burnt? Look, I burnt it!

In Chapter 5, we focus on boys' physical development and the value of active, challenging and adventurous play.

Chapter 6 draws on research that shows that early language development is influenced by the environment more than by sex differences, and offers practical ways to stimulate boys' language development.

In Chapter 7 we explore planned activities and rich experiences that support holistic learning in an inspiring and magical environment.

Finally, in Chapter 8, we focus on the physical environment, and suggest places and spaces that can be set up to provide adventure, challenge and possibility thinking.

Children should be able to have their personal 'eureka' moments, to achieve the unexpected and surprise and amaze themselves, and us! My hope is that the following chapters will offer practitioners ways to achieve this aim.

Creating an enabling learning environment for boys and girls

Introduction

> Jack, a sturdy 13-month-old, takes his fingers away from his mother's outstretched hands and balances precariously for a few seconds. He takes one step, and another, and another . . . until he is halfway across the room. As he takes his first steps, he holds his arms high up in the air and claps his hands above his head, smiling triumphantly.

Jack knows that he is making his own personal history, and he knows he is doing something momentous. Never mind Neil Armstrong's first steps on the Moon, here is Jack taking his very first independent steps on Earth! So what experiences did he have to give him the motivation, the confidence and the perseverance to take on the immense challenge of moving from a vulnerable newborn baby to a mobile toddler, in just over a year?

In this chapter, we explore this question by investigating how all children learn in the first few years of life, and we look at evidence that shows how learning dispositions impact on children's ability to learn. We also ask questions about similarities and differences in the way children develop and learn.

What do we know about how all children learn?

Learning from birth . . . early brain development

Lifelong cognitive and interpersonal skills are 'heavily shaped by learning'.

(Eliot 2012: 6, 7)

In the first years of life, the brains of babies and young children are developing at an astonishing speed, making 700 to 1,000 new connections every second. Early life experiences, including secure relationships and a stimulating environment, determine the healthy development of the young brain, while risk factors that restrict brain development include emotional stress, neglect and poor nutrition. The environment we provide for our youngest members of society, at home and in Early Years settings, is crucial.

At the age of 3 years, a child's brain is twice as active as an adult's brain and it has a remarkable plasticity – the ability to change in response to experience. Learning happens when synaptic connections are made between neurons, and plasticity allows the environment to sculpt young children's developing brains, influencing which connections are made, and which less well-used connections are 'pruned'.

Environmental factors influence *what children learn* – children's growing knowledge – and they also help establish *how children learn* – children's attitudes to learning and their beliefs about their identity within their family and in society. This places great responsibility on parents, carers and educators to be positive role models to young children and to be aware of some of the limiting messages that children meet as they step out into the world, so that they can counter them.

Social referencing: learning from other people

As children become increasingly socialised, they absorb messages at home from siblings, parents and the extended family, and then in the wider world from television, books and toy advertising, about how they should behave in order to gain approval. Nancy Stewart (2011: 39) describes this process as 'social referencing'.

Wesley, aged 8 months, is sitting in his high chair playing with a cardboard tube. He puts his mouth on one end and makes some sounds, then he loses interest and puts it down. His mother takes the tube and she makes some sounds into the end of the tube and offers it back to Wesley. He hesitates, then takes it and plays with it. Then he hands the tube back to his mother. She takes the tube and makes some sounds and hands it back to him. He watches her carefully, hesitates, then he 'sings' into the tube.

His mother claps delightedly, and they take turns singing into the tube.

This wonderfully positive interaction between Wesley and his mother is two-way, as his mother models social behaviour and Wesley responds in an early 'protoconversation' (Malloch and Trevarthen 2009), watching and taking turns. Wesley's enjoyment delights his mother, and Wesley responds to his mother's encouragement, strengthening the bond between them and encouraging Wesley to practise his new skill.

Through social referencing, children develop a belief system that influences how they respond to everyday experiences and more formal learning opportunities. Wesley is discovering that he can explore and experiment and try new things; he feels secure, knowing that his mother is there to share his learning and encourage him to try new things; learning isn't predictable in the big world that he is entering, but it is fun and safe and manageable.

Sadly, not all children receive positive messages and reinforcement of their behaviour. Compare Wesley's experience with that of Stevie:

> Stevie's mum came to pick him up from his day nursery. When he saw her, his eyes lit up and he ran towards her, waving a painting that he had done that afternoon.
>
> Stevie's mum gave the painting a quick glance and said: *It's a bit black, isn't it?*
>
> She lifted Stevie up and strapped him into his buggy, pushing the painting into her bag.

When we are conscious of the messages that children pick up through social referencing, we can use the plasticity of the young brain to protect the developing child against limiting and negative influences. Providing encouraging and positive influences helps children to build a positive self-identity and it broadens their options and learning opportunities.

Learning that 'I can': developing a sense of self-efficacy

> Arlo, aged 11 months, edges along a bench, holding on tightly as he isn't too steady on his feet yet. He's trying to reach his cup, which is at the far end of the bench. He takes a few steps, then he looks round at his mother to check that she's there. She smiles encouragingly so he edges further along until he reaches his cup. His mother celebrates with him: *Hey, you've done it! Well done!*

Balbernie (2011) emphasises the importance of this early phase of life for establishing powerful learning dispositions. Supported by his mother, Arlo is developing a sense of self-efficacy, which Bandura describes as a person's belief that they can make things happen (in Stewart 2011: 16).

Self-efficacy is a fundamental element of learning at any age. It challenges the view that ability is fixed and cannot be changed (Claxton 2008), and instead draws on the understanding that learning is a process which is challenging and involves hard work, even for exceptional achievers like Michelangelo.

If people knew how hard I worked to get my mastery, it wouldn't seem so wonderful at all.

(Michelangelo)

Children who have a strong sense of self-efficacy have an 'I can' attitude to learning. They derive satisfaction and intrinsic motivation from the process of learning and this lets them rise to challenges rather than being overwhelmed, even when learning is a struggle. They are willing to try new things and they are able to learn from mistakes.

Children with a weak sense of self-efficacy can find new learning daunting and are likely to give up when things become difficult. They believe that learning is a question of talent and ability: if they find learning difficult, they must lack ability, so there is no point in making an effort.

So how do children develop a strong sense of self-efficacy? Children learn a lot through mimicry, and positive self-efficacy is learned from positive role models in the context of an emotionally safe and structured environment with adults who show genuine interest and encouragement. Adult expectations of children also play an important role in children's developing belief system about their effectiveness as learners.

We saw how Arlo already has a strong sense of self-efficacy:

- He is secure enough to try new things, knowing that help is there if needed.
- He has been allowed to set his goal himself, and to achieve it in his own time.
- His mother shows that she has belief in his ability to achieve his goal.
- She encourages and praises him when he does things for himself, and when he achieves something new.

From home learning to school learning: some questions to consider

- Do the young children that you work with have equally strong male and female role models for learning? Are they more likely to see women than men reading and writing? (National Literacy Trust 2012)
- Do your children's parents have equal expectations for boys and girls in different areas of learning? Is there a general expectation that boys are better at tasks involving physical activity and dexterity, while girls are better at reading, writing and drawing?

Mindsets for learning: learning that 'I can get better at this, if I work at it'

Self-efficacy is one element in Carol Dweck's work on mindsets for learning. Babies are born knowing very little, but they have a vast capacity to learn and they aren't daunted by the size of tasks such as learning to talk or walk. Babies don't start off questioning if they have the innate talent and human qualities to be successful in the world. They rapidly pick up beliefs about their abilities as learners from people around them who reflect back at them: either 'you have the human qualities to learn all kinds of interesting skills and information'; or 'you don't have the human qualities to do very much with your life.' As we grow older, how many of us face the challenge of learning a foreign language with the ease that babies learn to talk?

Dweck (2012) identified two mindsets in her research into how children respond to new challenges in learning: a *growth mindset*, where children believe in their ability to achieve something new: 'If something is difficult, I must work harder and then I'll have learned something new.' In contrast, children might develop a *fixed mindset*, where new learning is perceived as being threatening and difficulties are seen as a reflection on the learner themselves: 'If something is difficult, I'm not very clever, so I might as well give up.'

Growth mindset: 'it's about learning'

Learners with a growth mindset:

- understand that learning involves hard work, not simply innate talent;
- see challenges as a vehicle for learning and growing;
- respond to feedback as a means of learning more and learning better;
- use setbacks as a way of identifying new areas for growth;
- enjoy learning from others;
- see achievement as the satisfying result of new learning.

Fixed mindset: 'it's about me'

Learners with a fixed mindset:

- believe that learning should come naturally, and if it doesn't, the person has no talent – therefore, effort is a waste of time;
- believe that learning new things is threatening and so it's to be avoided;
- respond poorly to feedback, which is seen as an attack on them as a person;
- find setbacks damaging and proof that they are not very clever;
- avoid learning from others, as this makes them feel inferior;
- see achievement as something that proves they are clever.

(Adapted from Dweck 2012)

(continued)

(continued)

Words associated with a growth mindset:	Words associated with a fixed mindset:
Do . . . stick at something . . . persevere	*Don't . . . try . . . fail*
Do . . . try new things . . . risk getting something wrong – the first time	*Avoid . . . new things . . . risks . . .*
Do . . . take on a challenge	*Avoid . . . making myself look silly*
Learning is enjoyable and I choose to do it	*Learning is stressful and I avoid it*

Mindsets are just beliefs. They're powerful beliefs, but they're just something in your mind, and you can change your mind.

(Dweck 2012: 16)

We can create an enabling environment that helps young children develop a growth mindset by building on their natural ability as babies to explore, experiment and revise their view of the world in response to experience. Before Jack could walk, he didn't think, 'I can't walk, I'm no good at walking – so I won't try.' He knew that he couldn't walk . . . yet. The key language is, 'I'm not very good at this . . . YET.'

From home learning to school learning: some questions to consider

- Is there a difference in the way that your boys and girls move from home learning experiences to school learning?
- Can you identify any gender influences in the way that boys and girls develop learning mindsets?

Self-regulation: learning that 'I can set my own goals and work out how to reach them'

Children who have a strong sense of self-efficacy and a growth mindset can develop *self-regulation* – a set of constructive behaviours and strategies that help them to become independent learners rather than being dependent on adult direction. Self-regulation involves having the self-awareness that allows us to stop doing something that we might want to do, but which we know impedes our effectiveness. For a young child, this might involve tuning out the distraction of another child's behaviour when he is listening to a story. It also can involve starting to do something, even if we might not want to do it. A young child might work hard to cut out an irregular shape for a class collage even though she finds it hard to use scissors, because she wants to contribute to the collage. Self-regulation is not the same as compliance, because the child's behaviour is linked to the task in hand, not to external expectations.

Self-regulation includes *executive function skills* that support the way we learn so that we can learn more effectively. Children who have well-developed executive function skills have a toolbox of learning strategies and dispositions, such as the ability to plan and make considered choices and decisions. They can test out their ideas in response to a hypothesis, and evaluate and adapt their ideas if necessary. They are unlikely to be compliant, and might question adults and ask for reasons why they are required to do something, seeking genuine responses from others. As they develop these skills, they can become independent and effective learners.

Children who don't have self-regulation skills find it harder to generate and try out new ideas. They are more likely to seek approval for their behaviour or their work and wait to be told what to do rather than being self-motivated and they find it hard to manage behaviour and persist in tasks.

Cody is sitting on the floor in his nursery classroom, building a tower with single Unifix cubes. He connects four, five, six cubes . . . and then the tower topples over. He tries again. Four, five, six, seven, eight cubes . . . and then the tower topples again. He repeats the process a few times, never managing to get higher than eight cubes. Then he has a thought. As he builds, he moves from sitting to crouching, so he gets taller as his tower gets higher. This time he manages 12 cubes before the tower topples.

Cody persists, moving from sitting to crouching to standing until his tower is nearly as tall as him. He stands triumphantly, holding the top of the tower with one finger and says: *Ta da!!*

Cody is totally focused on his task, maintaining concentration for about 15 minutes. He shows high-level executive function skills:

- He is self-motivated and has set his own goals.
- He is patient and determined.
- He shows problem-solving skills, trying different strategies and learning from experience.

Self-regulation skills can grow when children have space, time and encouragement to engage in individual tasks with self-set goals or in social, interactive and creative types of play, such as role play or collaborative and problem-solving play such as den-building. Children who spend time in open-ended, child-initiated activities in Early Years settings (rather than structured and time-limited activities set by others) are more able to set their own goals and determine how they reached them. Children learn to regulate their emotions and behaviour and to work independently and with others, developing and practising self-regulation skills.

From home learning to school learning: some questions to consider

- Where have you observed boys and girls demonstrating self-regulation skills?
- Have you noticed a link between boys' and girls' language skills and their self-regulation skills?

Conclusion

> Learning is about the way the world changes our mind, but our minds can also change the world.
>
> (Gopnik 2009: 8)

As children move from the home environment to the education system, they begin to meet learning targets that are set externally, rather than the intrinsic goals that they set themselves in their play. National assessment targets at the end of the Early Years Foundation Stage are set with uniform expectations of a 'good level of achievement' for cohorts of children rather than individual children, despite the fact that a cohort includes boys and girls with widely differing experiences, whose ages range across a full calendar year.

Early Years practitioners can provide an 'enabling environment' where all children can demonstrate the 'characteristics of effective learning' (EYFS 2012), when they observe children in their play and model positive social referencing and constructive feedback. Observations will show differences in the ways that boys and girls play. They will also show differences in the way that different girls play and in the way that different boys play. Through observational assessment and careful planning, practitioners can help all children to transfer and apply the self-regulation skills they show in their play-based learning to more adult-directed learning tasks, helping them to make academic progress as they move through the school system.

In the next chapter, we explore biological and environmental influences on boys' and girls' development, and consider how these might impact on the ways that boys and girls respond to the school environment and develop constructive learning dispositions.

Summary: helping children to become powerful life-long learners

Boys and girls are powerful learners from birth.

When they enter the education system, all children will learn more effectively if they have:

- **a sense of self-efficacy:** they believe that they can learn;
- **a growth mindset:** they believe that they can get better at learning;
- **self-regulation:** they believe that they can set and attain their own goals.

This happens:

- when the learning environment is set up in response to observational assessment;
- when children can spend time in self-directed activities that allow them to explore and experiment within agreed boundaries, and to negotiate rules;
- in an environment with non-prescriptive resources and plenty of time for child-initiated learning, where children can initiate ideas and make their own choices and decisions;
- when constructive feedback from adults and peers helps children to try new things, respond positively to mistakes, and make considered judgements about their work.

2

Pink, blue or purple
Gender identity and early learning

Introduction

When I was pregnant with my second child my daughter, then aged two and a bit, said she only wanted a baby sister. I didn't know if I was having a boy or a girl at the time but sensed trouble ahead, given that I only had a 50:50 chance of giving my daughter what she wanted. Then my wonderful midwife had a chat with my daughter, and said: 'so, if it's a baby boy, can I keep him?' Of course, my daughter wasn't going to let that happen, which was just as well, as she did have a baby brother.

Why was the sex of a newborn baby so important to such a young child and why is it the first thing that parents want to know? Knowing a baby's sex seems to set up immediate expectations of the new family life ahead. Most parents will say they don't mind if they have a boy or a girl, but imagine for the moment being pregnant with triplets. Would it make a difference if the babies were all boys or all girls? How might comments vary when prospective parents tell friends and family that they are having three boys . . . or three girls?

It's evident that men and women can, and often do, behave very differently, in all societies, and that behavioural differences can be observed between very young boys and girls. But what causes the differences in behaviour, and are there greater differences between the sexes or *within* groups of boys and girls, men and women?

This chapter explores two questions:

- Are observable differences in the behaviour of boys and girls biologically predetermined or the result of environmental influences?
- How can we mitigate any limiting impact of biological and environmental influences on gender identity?

1 Male and female differences: biology or environmental influences?

'Gender detectives'

> Rachel, age 8, and Simon, age 6, often play together happily as well as argue, as siblings do. They enjoy sharing books together, acting out stories with small world characters, playing in the park or creating a 'water Olympics' in the pool on holiday.
>
> When they went to a summer play scheme, they both found separate groups of friends, and told their parents about their day when they came home. Rachel had spent the day with a group of girls. They made up a play, and painted posters to advertise the play, as well as joining in with some organised craft activities. She told her mother the names of the girls that she had met, and lots of details about their lives, their brothers and sisters, their pets, their favourite toys. Simon had arrived in the hall and a football landed at his feet. He kicked it back and was immediately part of a large footballing mêlée that carried on until the end of the day. He told his mother what he'd had for lunch, and he knew the names of a few of the boys, but he hadn't picked up any detail about their lives. The boys' conversation had revolved around the football: *I'll go in goal. Man on! To me! Goal!!!!!!*

At home, Rachel and Simon's styles of play overlap and there are as many similarities in their behaviour as there are differences. At the play scheme, they conformed to common gender stereotypes. The question is, do children learn expected behaviour for boys and girls in social groups, or does an innate drive direct them towards gendered play? For parents and everyone who works with children, it is useful to identify and understand factors that we can't control – biology – as well as environmental factors that we can have some influence over. We can also consider ways to compensate for any clear biological differences, so that we can broaden all children's options, rather than reinforcing the differences.

Lise Eliot, a neuroscientist and expert on brain development and gender differences, argues that there are some small innate differences between boys and girls at birth and that these differences are 'amplified' by environmental influences, by society, which places great store on gender identity. She claims that innate differences are *small biases*, but they are not deterministic. We can compensate for the differences once we are aware of them, given the plasticity of the developing brain (Eliot 2012: 303), by ensuring that children have suitable opportunities to develop aptitudes that they might need to work a little harder to acquire. She also notes that there are greater differences *within* groups of boys and girls than *between* groups of boys and girls (Eliot 2012: 305).

Cordelia Fine describes children as 'gender detectives' from a very young age, checking out messages about the kinds of toys, clothes and behaviour that are 'for boys' or 'for girls' so that they can 'get it right' – in other words, they are looking for signals about behaviour that is socially acceptable (Fine 2011).

Neuroscience is still in its relative infancy and ambitious claims have been made about differences in the male and female brain that have been challenged equally robustly. However, we do know for certain that all experiences change the neural pathways in the brain, so when adults respond to infants according to gender stereotypes and when children identify and conform to gender stereotypical expectations, the behaviour they exhibit influences the way their brains develop.

What do we know about biologically predetermined sex differences?

'We have different roles, so we have different brains to fulfil these roles' (*Horizon* 2014). These are the words of an interviewee on a television programme that set out to investigate if male and female brains are hard-wired differently. It can be a comforting view, as it expresses the belief that there is a natural order to the world that we can understand, but that we can't challenge. But the fact that it is comforting does not make it true. There are research studies that show significant differences between male and female brains, but there have also been studies that have failed to replicate these findings. Neuroscientists warn against drawing generalised conclusions from single studies, and from our still limited knowledge of how the physical matter of the brain influences behaviour.

Paul Howard-Jones at the University of Bristol believes that inadequate communication between neuroscientists and educators is creating what he calls 'neuromyths' or 'neurononsense': claims that draw on generalisations and misinterpretations, but which are being used to influence classroom practice. Cordelia Fine goes a step further, using the term 'neurosexism' (Fine 2011), suggesting that beliefs about differences in the male and female brain are influenced by our beliefs about the role that men and women have in society. Brain scans show some physical differences between developing male and female brains, but we are still learning about how these differences translate into differences in behaviour. Men's brains are, in general, larger than women's brains, but men aren't more intelligent and some men's brains are smaller than some women's brains. There is less difference between the male and female brain than there is between male and female behaviour.

Neuroscience will have a lot to contribute to educators' understanding of how children learn, but it must be based on objective, evidence-based research, not claims that are not fully substantiated.

'Small biases'

If we put aside some very wide-ranging claims about sex differences, we can find a consensus on what 'small biases' in development between boys and girls look like – while accepting that there will always be some individual girls and boys who do not conform to the generalisations. We do know that:

Development at birth

- *At birth, boys' development lags behind that of girls*, and this makes them more vulnerable compared with girls, who are more resilient. Premature girls catch up developmentally with their peers more quickly than premature boys (Eliot 2012).

Development after birth

- *Boys mature more slowly in terms of language development, self-control and fine motor skills.* Higher levels of activity after birth mean that boys require more calories to survive and so are more vulnerable to poor nutrition (Eliot 2012).

Language development in boys and girls

- *Initially, there are small but identifiable verbal differences between boys and girls.* By the age of 6, there is no difference in vocabulary between cohorts of boys and girls (and men do as well as women in jobs that require them to be articulate and literate) (Eliot 2012).

Motor development

- *Gross motor: higher levels of activity after birth give boys more practice and help their gross motor development (sitting, standing, walking, climbing) and spatial abilities* (Eliot 2012).
- *Fine motor: boys develop fine motor skills more slowly than girls, and there is still a significant difference by the time children start nursery, pre-school and school.* Fine motor skills are needed for writing, drawing and tasks that involve small precise movements. Fine motor development also affects speech, which requires the ability to coordinate the small muscles in the throat, lips and tongue (Eliot 2012).

Hormonal differences

- *Testosterone: boys have higher levels of testosterone before birth and for the first six months of life but, after the first few months, 'there are virtually no differences between boys' and girls' levels of testosterone, estrogen, and other sex-related hormones until the onset of puberty'* (Eliot 2012: 87). It appears likely that prenatal testosterone and a brief testosterone surge immediately after birth have some influence on brain development and future gender-specific behaviour, but there is no hard evidence regarding the extent of its influence.

- *Cortisol: one research study showed that boys produce a greater surge of cortisol (a stress hormone) than girls when they are surprised or disturbed* (Eliot 2012: 74), contributing to their greater emotional fragility.

- *Inhibitory control: one of the greatest identifiable differences between boys and girls is in the development of inhibitory control, the ability to sit still and tune out distractions, which is slower to develop in boys.* Inhibitory control has been linked to stronger verbal skills as children use language to gain awareness and control, so boys who have less well-developed language skills might struggle to manage their behaviour (Eliot 2012).

Visual spatial skills or empathetic skills?

- *A number of research experiments have shown that men do slightly better at activities requiring visuospatial skills while women do slightly better at tasks that require the ability to read emotions from facial expressions.* These differences have been linked to prenatal testosterone levels, but it is also likely that the different skills have developed through practice, perhaps due to an initial bias towards physical activity or towards verbal interaction. Work by Gina Rippon (in Eliot 2012) has shown that, when tests for visual spatial ability were presented in a number of different ways, women did as well as men: that is, men and women can become better at certain tasks with practice.

The brief summary above shows that we know a little about reliable differences between male and female brains. Our challenge, as Early Years practitioners, as parents and as members of a society that aims to be inclusive, is to understand and respond to sex differences positively, without reinforcing and 'amplifying' them in individual children. The plasticity of the developing brain allows us to take conscious action to 'inoculate' boys and girls against the limitations of gender-stereotypical behaviour (Eliot 2012).

2 How can we mitigate any limiting impact of biological and environmental influences on gender identity?

How we treat 0–2-year-olds shapes their lives – and ultimately our society.

(Wave Trust/DfE 2013: 3, quoted in Dowling 2014: 6)

Picture a supermarket trolley with well-aligned wheels: it travels in a straight line and is easy to steer. Now picture a trolley with wheels that are just slightly misaligned. If we simply push it along, it will take us in an increasingly widening arc and we have to consciously and deliberately steer against its inclination if we want to determine where we go. We can think of sex differences in boys and girls as slight differences in the alignment of their 'wheels', which can be kept on track with some conscious effort, or can be allowed to move in an arc away from each other. When we challenge gender stereotypes, we act like the brain and muscles in a person steering a trolley with poorly aligned wheels: the brain decides the destination – a place where boys and girls have the same options and choices in their life – and the muscles take action to take the trolley where we want to go – the enabling environment.

Experiences and interactions affect the building of neural circuits in all developing brains, male and female, wiring the brain for language, cognitive, emotional and social skills. So early experiences are vital as they have the potential to exaggerate initial sex differences or counter any limitations. In the following case study, we focus in on language development, an area where boys often are observed to lag behind girls.

Context: a nursery class outdoor area

During a visit to a nursery class recently, I was in the garden when a girl called out to me: *What's your name?* She was playing with a group of girls on a climbing frame and they all leaned forward to join in the conversation. I told them my name, and asked their names. *I'm Charlotte Taylor Lottie. I'm called Lottie because there's another Charlotte in the class. Do you know Megan?* I asked if Megan is her sister. *Yes, she's in the other class.* The conversation carried on, and we talked about how old we both were, how many brothers and sisters we have both got, and if we are younger or older sisters. An adult called the children to join in an activity and conversation ended.

Not long after, a boy came rushing outside from the classroom, and jumped up three large stepped wooden blocks, followed by another boy. I noticed that they were wearing homemade wristbands, and made a comment: *You're wearing wristbands* . . . The first boy, Dexter, looked at me, smiled and leapt off the top step shouting *superpowers!* followed by his friend, Saul, who also made a superhero leap from the top step, shouting *superpowers!* Both boys disappeared across the garden.

From the above observation, we could conclude that the boys' language is less developed than that of girls of the same age, and that their social skills are also less developed. They chose to take their play away from the adult, after a brief interaction, while the girls chose to initiate and sustain a conversation. The danger is that this can become a self-fulfilling prophecy if practitioners choose to spend less time with the two boys, who are constantly on the move, than with the girls. Alternatively, we can compensate for small differences in language development, by making sure that additional time is given to encouraging boys to listen and express ideas, thoughts and feelings while valuing their interests and preoccupations.

The following observations are of two boys, Charlie and Simon, who are a year apart in age. Both children spend time with adults who listen to them, who wonder with them, who explain and question the world around them. Both children have a lot of talking practice and the simple equation of 'language in, language out' (Eliot 2012) has created confident children willing to grapple with complex ideas.

Charlie, age 2.10, is a scientist: *Let's investigate our drinks, mummy, by drinking them. Drink it mummy, drink it mummy, drink it mummy* . . .

He expresses himself creatively and poetically – driving through trees on a sunny day: *Mummy, the sun's blinking at me.*

He shows power of logical thinking:

Charlie's mother:	*What's that sound?*
Charlie:	*A pigeon, mummy.*
Charlie's mother:	*Where's it coming from?*
Charlie:	*A pigeon, mummy.*

Simon, age 3.10, broaches significant philosophical questions: *I can't wait to be dead.*

Simon's mother:	*Why?*
Simon:	*Then I won't have to keep tidying up.*
Simon's mother:	*I wonder what it's like, being dead* . . .
Simon:	*Well, you can't wriggle or eat. You just lie there.*

(continued)

23

(continued)

A year later, Simon, age 4.9, shows the capacity for abstract thought. He can imagine the world from the perspective of someone else and has the ability to express his thinking: *When you die it must seem as though the world has ended, but it hasn't really, because all the other people are still there.*

The fact that boys' development generally lags behind that of girls, and that they develop more slowly in the early years, clearly does not need to preclude boys from developing expressive language and thinking skills that equal the skills of many girls. Both girls and boys should have the right environmental influences and opportunities for their language and thinking to develop and to compensate for gaps and delays in development. Environmental influences that support language development are explored further in Chapter 6.

Gender-specific play

When Early Years practitioners are asked to make a list of words that describe the boys they work with, there is a remarkable consensus – the list inevitably includes words such as *noisy, boisterous, active, on the move, physical.* Boys' interests are described consistently as including *superheroes, space, dinosaurs, pirates or spies* . . . themes that involve action, teams and gangs, 'goodies' and 'baddies', conflict and resolution. Practitioners note that girls are much more likely than boys to sit at tables to draw and write, while boys are more likely to choose to spend time on a computer or playing outside. By the age of 4, observed differences are stark.

Gender-stereotypical play starts around the age of 1, and differences between boys and girls grow between the ages of 2 and 6, as children predominantly choose to play in same-sex groups. Boys and girls move in different directions in their play: girls' play commonly involves verbal negotiation and interaction, while boys' play emphasises physicality and competition (Eliot 2012: 153). Differing styles of play give boys and girls practice in different areas: girls tend to stay closer to an adult and look for approval more, helping their social and language skills develop (as we saw with Lottie and her friends); boys tend to play in larger, more active groups away from adults, supporting the development of spatial and gross motor skills (as we saw with Dexter and Saul).

The following case study is a reminder that we should be wary about how we interpret gender-stereotypical behaviour.

Arlo, aged 11 months, has just been given his first car, a chunky red one. He has become very skilful at crawling around using one arm, while he pushes the car with his free arm.

What is it about boys and cars, even at this age? his mum asks.

Is Arlo already a 'car-mad' boy? Let's look at what we *do* know about him…

He is an active child, interested in moving around, crawling from room to room, pulling himself up on the furniture, exploring a table leg, a book on the sofa, the pattern and texture in the upholstery before lowering himself down and setting off again across the room. When he is on the floor by his toy box, he sometimes has a peek inside, but quite quickly, he'll turn himself round and head off to explore his world again.

His red, chunky car fits into this scheme of play very well as it gives an additional dimension to his crawling. So, is it the car he's interested in, or the movement? If we decide it's the car, he'll be given more cars, and his play with wheeled vehicles will be reinforced by positive comments.

But let's watch him, on the floor while the shopping is being unpacked…

He spots a large packet of toilet rolls that has been put down on the floor. He crawls over and puts one hand on top of the packet, and off he goes, pushing the toilet rolls across the room.

If we assume that Arlo is 'car-mad' because he enjoys crawling and pushing cars, he will be given more cars and he will pick up social referencing cues that tell him that playing with cars is acceptable and appropriate behaviour. If we decide that Arlo loves being on the move and that's why he is drawn towards cars, he can also be given a doll's buggy or animals on wheels, and he can be taken to the park to enjoy moving on different surfaces and in different dimensions, up, along and through climbing apparatus and the natural environment. The challenge is to respond positively to all children's preoccupations but also to expand options for different types of play. Equally, a girl who spends less time physically exploring her environment can be encouraged to be more adventurous, to help her develop gross motor and visual spatial skills.

3 Practical ways to challenge gender stereotypes with young children

In Chapter 1, we saw how children use the process of social referencing as they learn to become part of their world. Social referencing helps children to become socialised, to develop a sense of belonging and learn behaviours that help them to be comfortable and accepted in their family and community. They also pick up implicit messages about society's expectations of appropriate behaviour for boys or girls. These messages are powerful, and are often transmitted unconsciously by the significant people in a child's life, amplifying the small and 'largely fixable' differences in the biology of boys and girls (Eliot 2012: 173).

It can be difficult to challenge gender stereotypes in home environments where children spend the majority of the time with their mother or other female carers and family members, and this is also true in Early Years settings, where the workforce is predominantly female. However, there are some things that we can do.

1   *Create a safe environment where staff and children can discuss and question their experiences and beliefs about gender stereotypes.*

Children explore and learn about the world in their stories and in their play. They can only reproduce the experiences they have had, and the models they have been given. Encourage children to reflect on their beliefs about gender identity and gender roles, at a time when they are developing an understanding of gender constancy. The understanding that boys will grow up to be men and girls will grow up to become women becomes secure by about the age of six years.

- Develop processes to ensure that staff and all children can and do challenge gender stereotypes (see Chapter 3).
- Challenge beliefs that involve judgements about the relative status of boys and girls, men and women – *Ben's mum is a doctor and Yasmin's dad is a doctor.*
- Discuss the things that children like and dislike and things that they are good at that overlap gender – *Kay loves playing on the swing in the park, and so does Jason.*
- Provide real-life role models that counter stereotypes and represent a range of behaviours – *talk about women's and men's football; give children models of women doing DIY jobs and men in caring roles; Robyn is a girl, and Tom's dad is called Robin.*

2   *Boys are not less capable – the role of adult expectations is key.*

Slower development at birth and in the first few years of life can lead to lower expectations of boys. We can remind parents that we want boys to become independent, practically and emotionally, so we should resist doing things for them that they can learn to do for themselves. If boys develop and mature more slowly, they need additional experiences to compensate, and expectations that are high but realistic:

- Adapt the learning environment to needs of all boys and girls.
- Have realistic expectations of children's attention spans, fine motor and verbal skills, and enhance children's development in these areas as they need these skills to progress in school.
- Encourage boys to talk about the things they can do. Promote self-competition rather than status-driven competition by celebrating children's 'personal best'.

Tyler has been watching some chicks hatch out in his classroom. He breaks off from his play to write a sign for the incubator: bee cefoo (be careful). He leans against the wall to write, then he tucks the pen into the loop on his trouser belt and runs off.

Celebrate achievements and make a display with photographs of the things that children can do:

'I can . . . get dressed . . . remember my wellies . . . tidy up . . . cut up my apple . . . pour my water . . . feed the rabbit . . . draw my mum'.

3 *Avoid giving a higher status to either gender.*

When Angus's mother picked him up from nursery, he was drinking from a pink trainer cup. She immediately took it away from him. 'His Daddy wouldn't like it', she explained to his keyperson.

Some parents suppress boys' interest in what they perceive to be girls' toys or girly colours such as pink. If the female world is seen as being lower status than the male world, fathers can worry that their boys will be disadvantaged in a high-status, male competitive world if they show an inclination towards what they perceive to be feminine behaviour. Boys pick this message up early (by the age of 2–3) and typically reject toys that are represented as being 'girly'. Girls, however, are less likely to reject 'boys' toys, so they have access to a wider choice of toys.

- Make sure that girls' and boys' styles of play and learning are valued equally.
- Find ways to make all toys inviting to boys and girls, by offering open-ended play opportunities that allow all children to make choices based on their personal preferences and not on gender stereotypical expectations to give all children access to a wider range of toys.
- Talk to parents about their expectations of gender-appropriate behaviour and toys.
- Interact with children and parents and carers to model more egalitarian behaviour.
- Challenge any language or behaviour that represents girls as weak and 'sissy'.
- Challenge any language or behaviour that represents boys as aggressive and less good at reading and writing.

4 *Check how all areas of provision are used to see if they are inviting for boys and girls.*

5 *Check your resources – books, small world, posters, computer games – to ensure that they provide positive and enabling images of men and women, boys and girls.*

6 *Use inclusive language – children, rather than boys and girls, families or parents rather than mums and dads.*

Conclusion

In the next chapter, we focus on the learning environment that children will meet when they start at nursery, pre-school or school, aged 6 months, or 2, or 4 years old. We explore practical ways in which adults can set up the learning environment to scaffold and teach self-regulation behaviours and strategies in learners. As Early Years practitioners, we can work with the powerful learning mechanism that is the young child, making it a safe, joyful and stress-free experience while supporting their dispositions to take on a challenge. We can also be very conscious of messages that we are giving children about what is normal and acceptable for girls and boys in terms of their behaviour.

Summary

We don't want to limit children's (and adult's) choices.

If sex differences are biologically determined, practitioners should know about biological differences.

But:

- we should be conscious of the plasticity of the developing brain and its susceptibility to environmental influences – positive and negative;
- we should be aware that there are more similarities than differences between the sexes;
- we must be careful not to generalise about all boys, or implement strategies aimed at all boys rather than individual children;
- we must be careful not to blame and limit our expectations of boys because of behaviour that is socially constructed.

3 | Pushing back the boundaries for learning

Introduction

> Max, age 4, reaches up to put a heavy basket on a self-service till in the supermarket. His mother calls him and tells him to bring the basket to a till where someone can check out their shopping. *Oh,* he groans. *That's no fun.*

Max is telling us a lot about how children learn best. He wants to be busy, be active, he doesn't want to wait passively. If he had been able to use the self-service check-out, he would have had fun scanning the items and watching the screen, and he would also have learned about size, weight, numbers, cause and effect, while developing fine motor skills, confidence in his abilities – and much more – in a situation that had genuine purpose for him. He seemed to know that, asking for what he needed to learn.

In previous chapters, we reflected on the significance of dispositions, skills and strategies in helping children like Max to become powerful learners, and we explored some similarities and some differences in the ways that boys and girls develop and learn.

In this chapter, we consider how we can minimise the difference in attainment between boys and girls when they start school, as boys consistently do less well, with 69 per cent of girls and 52 per cent of boys achieving a good level of development in all areas of learning at the end of the EYFS (DfE 2014b). We explore ways to establish a safe and secure learning environment with clear and firm boundaries and expectations for behaviour, allowing us to expand the boundaries and expectations for learning so that boys and girls can have space to play and learn in ways that respect their similarities and differences: boys can be boys, but more importantly, children can be children.

1 Creating an inclusive learning environment for boys and girls

Early learning experiences at home

In the first years of life, children have widely varying experiences at home and with the people who care for them, experiences that influence how they are able to respond to the learning environment that they meet when they start in an Early Years setting. EPPE research into the effects of pre-school education (Sylva et al. 2004) demonstrates the importance of the home learning environment (HLE) in influencing all aspects of children's development and learning, including social and behavioural development. Some children will have taken part in everyday activities, such as cooking, simple household repairs or putting washing in the washing machine alongside their parents and carers, unconsciously absorbing language, mathematical concepts and fundamental scientific principles. Some children will be very familiar with books and stories, and some will be less so. Some children will have formed strong and secure relationships with their caring adults so that they are ready to step out into the world outside the home, while others have been less fortunate and experience the world as a threatening place with dangers to be avoided or navigated. In addition to these wide-ranging differences, girls and boys experience the world in different ways from birth, in our highly gendered society. All of these environmental factors interplay with each child's unique personal development at a time when the developing brain is most plastic and responsive to experience.

Academic versus intellectual learning

Despite each and every child's individuality, when children start in Early Years settings, they are immediately grouped into learning 'batches' according to the date of their birth, and all channelled along a path towards the same externally determined learning targets. The aim is to improve all children's life chances by compensating for environmental factors that disadvantage some children, but there are dangers in measuring all children against identical criteria when the children themselves are so different. Inevitably, some children will fail and some children will succeed when they are presented with a fixed curriculum that doesn't take into account their different stages of development, experiences and preoccupations.

Katz argues that increasingly narrow and prescriptive 'academic' teaching is having harmful long-term consequences, as it can stifle the 'intellectual dispositions' that will support children's learning throughout their lives. While some academic instruction is necessary to support children's investigations, this must be balanced against children's holistic development and innate learning dispositions (Katz 2015).

In the supermarket, Max had a playful situation taken away from him. He lost the initiative and therefore he lost interest when he could no longer use the self-service checkout. In formal, academic classrooms, children can lose their intellectual curiosity and initiative. Over time, many children learn to conform and respond to targeted, assessment-led instruction and achieve well in a group, but other children are failed by the system when they struggle to make sense of the formal instruction. Boys in particular are more likely to struggle in a formal setting (Cigman 2014), but all children learn better when their natural curiosity is harnessed to develop their intellectual capabilities (Katz 2015).

Why do some boys do less well than girls when they start school?

Jon is sitting at a table writing numbers on a whiteboard. He is left-handed and his pencil control is weak, so his teacher has given him a whiteboard to encourage him to have a go and wipe off any attempts that he feels aren't good enough. He sits at the table with hunched shoulders copying the number 8, wiping it off with his hand, and repeating this over and over. His teacher comes over to him after about ten minutes, sees his pen-stained hand and his blank whiteboard, and tells him he can go out to play.

Young children form their self-identity in relation to people around them, and as they move away from their family into a group setting, they need to see positive images of themselves reflected back at them. Struggle in learning can be positive, but if children struggle with their learning, and this struggle isn't dealt with constructively to create a 'growth mindset' (Dweck 2012), these children can form a negative image of themselves, as we see with Jon. He is in danger of seeing himself as less intelligent and less able to learn, even though he simply doesn't have the fine motor control to form the number shape 'yet'.

Boys' slower physical and emotional maturation can be highly significant when children enter formal schooling, reinforced by the small but noticeable developmental differences between boys and girls that we explored in Chapter 2.

- **Language:** small differences in early language development between boys and girls can have a lasting impact if differences are seen as a measure of a child's ability rather than experience. This can influence the expectations that Early Years practitioners have of children, often unconsciously, and low expectations can lead to lower achievement. Eliot (2012: 237) refers to this as the 'stereotype threat'.

- **Fine motor skills:** young boys' slightly less well-developed fine motor skills can make the physical act of writing, drawing and recording numbers challenging, and even painful. Boys might struggle more than girls with self-care skills, such as dressing themselves and cutting up food. Children tend not to choose to do things they find difficult, so they have less practice developing their fine motor skills.

- **Gross motor skills:** the milestones of gross motor maturation are an exception to boys' overall slower maturation from birth as boys stand, crawl, walk and run at a similar age to girls. By pre-school years, boys tend to be stronger and more mobile and they like to practise these skills. As they have more practice, they improve their gross motor skills even further.

- **Inhibitory control:** boys' later development of inhibitory control can impact on their social development and on their ability to conform to classroom expectations. More boys than girls are identified as having behaviour problems and learning difficulties and more boys than girls are excluded, even before the age of five (Morton 2015).

- **Styles of play:** although there are many overlaps in the ways that boys and girls choose to play, the type of play that many boys choose to engage in – boisterous, active, noisy, involving movement – is likely to contribute to some boys' struggle to adapt to and thrive in Early Years classrooms, where children are expected to sit at desks or in group activities for much of the day.

In group settings, children become increasingly conscious of their status in relation to their peers, and it can be very uncomfortable for status-conscious, competitive boys to see other children being praised and rewarded for doing things that they find difficult. The danger is that these children become 'fixed mindset' children who stop trying to learn (Dweck 2012).

2 Safety to explore and take risks

> Children should be able to play *'bravely and adventurously'*.
>
> (MacMillan, quoted in Broadhead et al. 2010: 71)

Creating a physically and emotionally secure environment

All learning involves some element of risk-taking and children are better able to take risks if they have physical and emotional security from which they can explore and try new things. Gopnik (in Gopnik et al. 2007) talks of 'an invisible bungee cord' between mother and toddler, and in Early Years settings, this needs to be recreated, so that children can explore, and then come back to a caring adult who provides a safe reference point.

> Children learn to be strong and independent through positive relationships.
>
> (EYFS 2014: 6)

We can give children the best foundation for life by allowing them to explore the world from the fresh, exciting and developmentally appropriate perspective of a small child while supporting them to take secure next steps in their learning and development.

This happens best not in a controlling environment where adults guide each and every step a child makes, but in a flexible, stimulating environment where all children can experience excitement and joy, where they can choose where and how they play alongside adults who help give learning a genuine purpose.

So how can we give children more freedom to learn and develop: the freedom that boys appear to crave and that girls need too? Simon Carr (2001: 7) brought up two boys in an all-male household, as a sole parent after the death of his wife. He explored the issues of boundary-setting as a parent, with findings that are equally relevant in an Early Years setting. He introduced 'fewer rules . . . but bigger rules'. He recognised that the more rules that are created, the more there are to be broken, which results in behaviour that is seen as unacceptable, because it has broken the rules. But what if some of the rules are unnecessary? Having fewer rules resulted in fewer incidences of wrongdoing and less need for constant sanctions. But the rules that he did set were sacrosanct and were enforced absolutely. 'The boys have very definite limits that they mustn't go beyond. Inside the perimeter they can do very much as they please, but they must stay inside the boundaries.'

Creating a physically secure learning environment

We can reproduce Carr's approach in Early Years classrooms. We don't need a lot of rules as long as the rules that we do have are consistently applied. Waller et al. (2010) argue that risk reduction comes through a decision-making process that is based on pedagogical understanding of the environment alongside adult support that allows children to recognise and assess risk.

Ground rules relating to physical security will regulate behaviour to ensure that children stay safe and that they don't risk the safety of others, while allowing them to take calculated risks and explore their physical world.

Children need to be protected from serious injury, but a highly controlled environment where risk is eliminated only keeps children safe in the short term, as it doesn't allow children to learn to weigh up and assess risks and learn their limitations and their abilities. 'Risk perception is like a muscle that needs to be developed and flexed' (Blincoe 2015). When children meet small but real risks, they can experience the pleasure of pushing their personal boundaries, challenging themselves and learning a new skill, such as safe climbing or balancing on a beam.

A hazard is something a child does not see.
A risk is a challenge a child can see and chooses to undertake or not.
Eliminating risk leads to a child's inability to assess danger.
(Sign displayed in a children's centre, available from
https://twitter.com/Elizabeth Jarman, 2 November 2014)

Risk–benefit assessments are now being used in many local authorities, 'whereby both risks and benefits are assessed and decisions made as a result of weighing up both factors' (Moss 2012: 15).

> **Scenario:** In a Danish kindergarten, children are allowed to climb a tall tree in the garden when they know that they can climb down as well as up. Children start cautiously, climbing a few steps, and as they grow in confidence, they learn to judge their own limits, assess the risks and push themselves further. Repetition and practice helps them to become better climbers and better at assessing risks.

The risk–benefit assessment in this case requires the adults:

- to set clear ground rules to ensure safe climbing;
- to teach explicit skills that are needed to climb, following the child's lead;
- to observe individual children so that they know if a child is likely to put themselves into a dangerous situation;
- to assess the physical environment, to make sure that there is no risk of serious injury from broken glass, for example, or sharp stones under the tree. The tree is always within the sightlines of an adult.

> **The risks:** falling and getting a cut or graze; breaking a limb.
>
> **The benefits:** physical exercise; learning about what their body can do and its limitations; developing an awareness of their place in space; coordination; social and emotional development; rising to a challenge; learning about nature; learning to assess danger.
>
> **The reality:** no child in the kindergarten has had a serious injury from climbing the tree.

Children tend to underestimate their abilities rather than taking unsafe risks and they look out for each other, telling a friend to stop or helping them to find a foot or hand-hold, in an environment where this is encouraged. As children repeat an activity, they become braver and extend the degree of challenge, but they do this in small steps. It's a dynamic process that takes place over time as they grow and develop new physical skills and they develop the ability to deal with failure and take on new challenges at their own rate and with different degrees of support.

Emotional security in the learning environment

Once the behavioural boundaries and expectations are established, we can also create ground rules that give children emotional security to:

- take risks in their thinking, ask unusual questions and explore the world of ideas, alongside adults and children who listen to each other and support each other to take steps into the unknown. Children and adults are free to question and challenge each other's thinking, respectfully, without being judgemental of the person;
- allow each child to be individual in a group, who can choose to work alone or alongside other children and adults, collaborating and respecting each other's views and ideas.

Babies are born with powerful learning strategies. They watch their carers intently and learn how to interpret responses, before beginning to initiate interactions that will help them to comprehend their personal identity and the boundaries between themselves and other people and to form social relationships. They learn to kick and stretch and roll, to reach out, to touch and drop things, developing the muscle strength and hand–eye coordination that they need to move around in the world, discovering their own physical strengths and boundaries.

When the right environmental factors are in place, babies develop into young children who go on using these powerful learning strategies, flexibly adapting them to new situations as they meet them. In the EYFS, these strategies are called *the characteristics of effective learning*.

Children need emotional and intellectual security to maintain the characteristics of effective learning once they start in a group setting. This security comes from a strong sense of belonging and a secure sense of identity, and this in turn comes from secure attachments with a key person and other significant adults.

Emotionally secure children who experience 'companionable learning' (Roberts 2014) are able to develop a sense of agency, learning that their actions make a difference to their own lives and the lives of others. This can come about through episodes of 'well-being' play and learning alongside an involved companion, in real-life and imaginative play situations. It can also develop when children experience the joys of having sustained time to be on their own as well as with others, to follow their preoccupations, before sharing their experiences with a companion. Children experience intellectual security when they know that they are being listened to and that they are trusted to make considered decisions.

Balancing structure and risk

Tovey (in Broadhead et al. 2010) explores Early Years practitioners' attitudes to risk and uncovers a wide range of tolerance levels of risk. It is absolutely understandable that practitioners are safety-conscious. Risk management is a shared responsibility and it is vital that teams meet regularly:

- to establish the pedagogical value of risk-taking in learning – the benefits to the children;

- to agree the boundaries and expectations that underpin the ground rules of the settings;

- to agree and review ground rules and the specific language used with the children and with parents and carers, to ensure that children experience consistency;

- to share and support each other when individuals experience difficult and challenging scenarios.

The experience of many Early Years practitioners (Cigman 2014) has shown that boys become highly motivated learners in physically and emotionally secure environments that allow them to be active and challenge themselves physically.

Children who experience physical, emotional and intellectual security can explore and experiment in their physical and social surroundings, learn to interact socially and emotionally with new and familiar adults and children, and extend the boundaries of their cognitive understanding by asking questions, trying things out, getting things wrong and trying something new. In this way, children develop a positive sense of themselves as 'mastery' learners, and they become more competent and more able thinkers.

We can help children to understand adult expectations and to allow them to become more comfortable in a group by setting very clear and explicit boundaries and expectations. This is true for boys and girls, but Biddulph (2003) suggests that boys especially need to experience a clear structure, with someone clearly in charge in order to feel secure enough to become confident learners.

3 Practical ways to set appropriate boundaries and expectations

Four boys were having enormous fun piling small wooden bricks into a large trug, and tipping them out. One boy climbed inside the trug, and the others delighted in covering him with bricks, right up to his face. They were clearly conscious of safety, as no one threw bricks or handled them inappropriately, and one boy said 'gently' to one of the others. They all wanted a turn in the trug, and no one had to go in or stay in there for longer than they wanted to.

The play described above might challenge some practitioners' tolerance of risk, but close observation of the play showed it to be very regulated, although the rules were rarely stated explicitly. The children were having a huge amount of fun and were highly motivated. They were honing their fine motor skills as they placed the bricks into the trug. They were absorbing mathematical concepts of space, size, quantity, mass and volume. They were experiencing the physics of balance and counter-balance. They were able to take turns and play collaboratively. They used language to give instructions and to describe what was happening.

The children were able to have a lot of freedom, because the scenario took place in a classroom where there were secure boundaries and expectations. The children had been involved in negotiating and agreeing ground rules at the beginning of the year, helping them to appreciate that the rules were for everyone's benefit, giving them a sense of belonging. This helped them learn to regulate their behaviour so that they were able to engage in boisterous play safely.

When adults see children becoming more confident and capable of self-regulating, they can become less risk-averse.

Setting ground rules

- *Ground rules should be clear and explicit to help children regulate their behaviour.*

  Young children use 'private speech' (Vygotsky 1987), a monologue or commentary on their play and behaviour and, over time, this becomes an internal monologue that helps children make decisions about how to act and behave. Children with lower language skills and less private speech can find it harder to self-regulate.

- *Establish rules that are developmentally appropriate.*

  Check children's understanding of the rules. There is no point in telling a 2-year-old that they must share before they are at a developmental stage where they understand what this means, but it is possible to set up a system where children can start to learn about sharing. Use a timer for turn-taking, for example on the computer or on bikes. Have cooperative toys such as bikes and blocks, to develop a collaborative ethos. Have adequate resources so that all children can find something interesting to do.

- *Negotiate positive ground rules.*

  Give reasons for the rules in consistent and repeated language that children can understand. Listen to children and respect their views, while ultimately having the final word.

- *Agree ground rules as a team.*

  This ensures a common response from all adults, practitioners and parents, especially in sensitive situations.

- *Be consistent in applying the rules.*

  Children use 'social referencing' (Stewart 2011) to learn about the rules and expectations that are acceptable in a learning environment that has been created for the group, not for them as individuals. Ground rules can help children to feel comfortable within a group identity, while allowing them to express themselves as an individual.

- *Clarify routines* to support children who struggle with transitions, such as tidy-up time or moving away from a group activity to free-flow play.

- *Set ground rules in a way that matches children's play and interests.*

> ## Ground rules for superheroes on the move
>
> Look before you leap!
>
> Fly, but not too high.
>
> Observe the speed limit.
>
> Friends to the rescue.
>
> Superheroes look after the innocent.

Boundaries and expectations should be flexible enough to account for different styles of play and a range of children's typical behaviour and, once they have been agreed, they become non-negotiable.

Establishing a code of behaviour

He's a classic boy: wriggling and jiggling!
The boys often found it hard to concentrate during adult-led activities.

(Cigman 2011)

We know that young boys can be noisy, boisterous and active, as this stereotypically boyish behaviour is very visible and hard to ignore. What is causing the behaviour?

Boys have more muscle bulk and higher levels of testosterone than girls as a rule, which can lead to competitive behaviour and the need to be physically active. With help, children can come to understand that certain behaviour can be acceptable in one situation (for example, using loud voices or running outside) while being unacceptable in another situation (the same behaviour indoors). A clear and explicit behaviour code can help children to manage and control their own behaviour once they understand and can articulate the reasons for the rules. Children can understand that behaviour is inappropriate if it:

- hurts someone else, another living creature or themselves;
- damages the physical environment;
- interferes with another child's play or learning.

However, some behaviour that is perceived as being challenging in a group context can simply be age-related, developmentally appropriate behaviour. Sitting still for more than a few minutes at carpet time is hard for most 2-year-olds, and it can be hard for many 3 to 5-year-olds. Children need to move in order to develop a strong vestibular (balance) system, and the kind of restless, fidgety behaviour that young children commonly show is telling us that they are not spending enough time moving.

Helping children to learn the code of behaviour

> My children always obey me. And the reason is that I find out what it is that they
> want to do and then advise them very strongly to do it.
>
> (President Edgar J. Hoover, quoted in Carr 2001: 8)

Young children learn that the familiar expectations of their home environment can be different from the expectations of an Early Years setting, where they must become part of a new collective identity. Many children are skilled at observing and processing signals that tell them how they should behave and if adults approve of their behaviour. They learn to imitate the behaviour of people who are their role models, and this behaviour is reinforced by rewards, sanctions and punishments in what Bandura termed the social learning theory (Bandura 1977). But some children take time to understand that the teacher is the appropriate role model in a classroom. It can be hard for some children to pay attention to an adult when another child is doing something interesting (but possibly less appropriate) and these children will take longer than others to develop socially acceptable behaviour. This might be because they haven't had a consistent code of behaviour established at home, or they might lack the language skills or self-calming skills needed to process, express and manage emotions: skills that typically develop later in boys.

A child who struggles to understand why some behaviour is acceptable and other behaviour is unacceptable can't make changes to gain the adult's approval. A child who doesn't understand, or isn't able to meet the expectations, is likely to withdraw, become disruptive or become over-compliant.

> Jamie: *When I get really angry I turn into a dinosaur, when I'm angry and sometimes
> I chase people.*

In the school year 2013–14, boys were three times more likely than girls to be permanently excluded from nursery or reception classes (Morton 2015). We know that boys find it harder than girls to regulate their behaviour in a social setting, so it is important to be very clear and specific in the way we establish a code of behaviour:

- *Model and explain appropriate behaviour in everyday situations:* for example, agree with the children that they look at books on the sofa in the book area, rather than engaging in rough and tumble play.
- *Explore and agree different ways of behaving at group or circle times:* for example, use persona dolls to discuss and problem-solve scenarios relating to inappropriate behaviour.
- *Remind children of the rules and expectations clearly and positively:* 'Remember we walk inside.'

- *Give positive feedback about the child's behaviour as well as responding to negative behaviour:* help children learn to articulate their feelings and explain why they should behave differently.

- *Enforce the rules and behaviour, but don't punish the child.*

- *Support parents* who might be struggling to enforce clear boundaries and expectations at home. Sharing the ground rules of the setting can provide security for a child who is receiving mixed or unclear messages about their behaviour. The key person can provide a link with the child's family, discussing socio-cultural differences in expectations and enforcement of behaviour in a non-judgemental way.

> Boys' physical and active learning style has been incorporated into the planning and continuous provision.
>
> (Oxfordshire Boys' Writing Project 2009–10)

Conclusion

In this chapter we have explored ways of creating a safe and inclusive learning environment, recognising the small but potentially significant developmental differences between boys and girls. We show how boys can be supported to integrate into a group setting while retaining their individual character and learning styles by creating explicit boundaries that keep all children safe. Within these boundaries, boys can become active risk-takers, enjoying a large degree of freedom that will give them a sense of infinite possibilities.

The next chapter investigates practical ways to set up the learning environment to give children greater freedom to be adventurous.

Summary

- Establish boundaries and expectations that help children to feel physically and emotionally safe without eliminating choice and challenge.

- Share the boundaries and expectations to help children develop a strong self-identity and a sense of agency as learners.

- Be aware of the 'stereotype threat' that can limit children's options in their play.

- Provide children with a wide range of opportunities for learning that avoid gender-stereotyping and allow them to try out new identities as they play.

In short: *let boys be boys, let boys be children and let children learn like children.*

4 Creating irresistible spaces for play and learning

Introduction

In the previous chapter, we considered the importance of establishing a safe and secure physical and emotional environment for boys and girls, based on our understanding of how children typically develop and learn. We explored ways to enhance the environment to account for the specific developmental needs of some boys who need additional support for their language development, fine motor development and their ability to regulate their learning and behaviour in a group setting. This chapter shows how we can:

- observe children to determine how developmentally appropriate the environment is, and how well it motivates children to learn through their play;
- set up a physical environment that allows boys to be confident, active learners, and that encourages girls to be confident and active learners as well;
- tune into the interests of boys so that we can provide stimulating spaces and resources for all children;
- offer adult support to prompt new investigations and support children's exploratory play and learning.

1 Getting the environment right for boys – and girls

Practitioners often describe boys as being more challenging than girls in a school context. But, instead of regarding boys as the challenge, the challenge can be to adapt the environment to the boys, rather than expecting boys to adapt to the environment, by creating an environment that values and encompasses the way that young boys commonly learn. Boys who struggle in a prescriptive and controlling environment can flourish and grow in environments that are flexible and responsive to individuals, and small developmental differences between boys and girls don't need to become a problem. This kind of classroom benefits all children, boys and girls, but small-scale action research in settings that focused on supporting boys' learning has shown that boys particularly benefit from these conditions (Cigman 2014).

Ferre Laevers has devised a set of well-being and involvement scales for practitioners to use to evaluate how children in their settings are feeling and how engaged they are in their activities (Laevers 2005). Involvement scales measure concentration levels in an activity, recognising that deep-level learning happens when children display high levels of involvement.

Involvement scales help practitioners to measure the following qualities:

- motivation;
- intense mental activity;
- satisfaction;
- exploratory drive;
- the degree of challenge: are children at the limits of their capabilities?

Well-being scales help practitioners to measure the following qualities in children:

- enjoyment;
- relaxing and inner peace;
- vitality;
- openness;
- self-confidence;
- being in touch with oneself.

In short, well-being is about the 'quality of life'. It refers to an optimal relation between the child and its environment.

(Laevers 2005: 9)

How do we know if we have created the environment right for children?

We can evaluate how well the learning environment is set up to promote well-being and involvement by stepping back and observing children as they access provision.

Observation: Oska is nearly three and half and goes to his village pre-school five mornings a week.

Oska is playing in the home corner: *Rrrrr . . .*

He shakes his whole body and flops down on the floor in a heap. He wanders around the room, goes back to the home corner and flops down again onto the carpet.

After a few minutes, he gets up and wanders across the room and 'play punches' Barney, making a loud punching sound.

Oska: *You're dead.*

Both boys 'play shoot' each other with their fingers, making shooting noises, lying down and jumping up. Then the two boys start 'play shooting' two girls, who ignore them.

After a few minutes, Oska stops the 'shooting' actions and goes to the book corner. He lies on the floor, and drives a toy car up the side of the sofa making car noises, drops the car, rolls on the floor, lies still for a few minutes, then gets up. He looks around, goes to the home corner and lies down on the ground.

He gets up and goes and sits on a chair. Alice walks past and Oska roars at her. Alice jumps, then moves away.

Oska picks up a Sticklebrick 'gun', and starts play fighting with Barney.

Oska: *Barney, Barney, Barney, when I shoot you, you have to go down. Barney, Barney, Barney, let's go over here where no one can see us.*

The two boys go into a hidden corner.

An adult comes over and asks them what they are playing.

Oska: *We're doctors.* Both boys make gun sounds and a shooting action with their finger.

Barney: *Mine goes 'mug pwshhhh . . .'*

What is the relationship between Oska and his environment in this observation?

Oska's behaviour tells us that his levels of well-being and involvement are low. He moves between withdrawn behaviour and mild aggression and he is unable to settle to anything or sustain any activity. He has no conversations with other children or adults and chooses to isolate himself in a hidden corner of the room. He shows little motivation or satisfaction in anything that he does and he doesn't smile once during the observation, which lasts for about 20 minutes. Oska's low levels of well-being and involvement might reflect personal issues, or they might reflect a need to improve the environment so that it matches the learning needs of all children more successfully. Further observations of other children in all areas of provision over time would give a fuller picture.

There is consistent evidence to show that boys settle more slowly than girls into Early Years settings and that practitioners voice more concerns over boys' behaviour and attainment (MacLure and Jones 2009). Observations in a number of projects that focused on supporting boys' learning showed that boys provide a good barometer of the quality of the learning environment (Cigman 2014). When the environment was too restrictive or expectations weren't clear, boys were more likely than girls to express their discomfort, either through noisy and boisterous behaviour or by withdrawing. Boys became more confident and competent learners when simple changes were made to the learning environment, to give children the freedom to explore, experiment, follow their interests and persist in their learning over time, and when adults gave children constructive and encouraging support within the safe and secure boundaries that we examined in Chapter 3.

2 Matching provision to the learning styles and interests of boys

In this section we consider simple steps that we can take to evaluate and create the 'optimal relation' between the learning environment and boys. By stepping back, observing the children and evaluating provision, we can bring theory and practice together, ensuring that our provision reflects our knowledge about how boys learn best.

Step one: observe boys' play in the whole setting

Where do the boys choose to go? Are there adequate opportunities for peer and adult interaction and stimulating cross-curricular learning in the places that they choose to go?

Where do adults spend most of their time? Do adults spend as much time engaging constructively with the boys as with the girls?

Are there places where the boys rarely go? Does this limit their access to any areas of the curriculum? For example, do they tend to spend most of their time outside, and if so, do adults plan and support activities equally inside and outside?

Are there areas of provision where well-being and involvement levels are noticeably high or low?

Step two: observe individual boys

What do your observations tell you about individual boys' interests, capabilities and styles of play?

- What are they doing and saying?
- What are they playing with?

- What are they most interested in?
- Is their play challenging and engaging?
- What are they really good at?

Boys' play often involves power relationships between 'goodies' or superheroes and 'baddies', setting up a pecking order by deciding who is going to be a goodie or a baddie, a chaser or one of the chased. In her discussion of boys' play, Jarvis notes the prevalence of language that Jordan (1995) has called 'warrior discourse' (Jarvis in Broadhead et al. 2010: 63), language that reflects a fascination with danger, magic, physical competition, special skills and status:

> 'He's going to kill us!'
>
> 'Hey, I'm going to kill you!'
>
> 'Hey, get away from my sword!'
>
> 'Guess what, you can't ride on scorpions can you? Look, I'm standing on one. 'Cos I make it dead.'
>
> 'I got powers! I can turn into Batman! AND Spiderman!'

Language is often clipped and action-focused:

> 'Come on guys! Blog station! Let's go to the blog station! Aaah . . . Quickly! Let's run!'
>
> 'I'm making a window . . . I'm making a chocolate cake . . . I'm making a door . . . I winned!!'

Other themes that can be observed involve a fascination with breaking rules and exploring dangers from the comfort and security of a familiar space:

> Steffan and Zak are digging in the sandpit in the nursery outside area.
>
> Steffan: Digging for treasure, are we?
>
> Zak: No, we're making dangerous stuff.
>
> Steffan: Are we making concrete to get bad guys?
>
> Zak: Yes, that's why we need dangerous stuff to get concrete.
>
> Steffan: Zak, watch me, we're making dangerous stuff to kill bad guys.

Boys' play can contain implicit rules, exciting possibilities and demonstrate the ability of children like Fergus, in the observation below, to form a logical and creative plan (to make a slippery mountain). It can also be harder to manage, as boys' play is often very fluid physically. The challenge is to engage with aspects of boys' play as they whizz past!

Context: the reception teacher explains to the children that they can make a role-play cake shop.

Hannah: *A cake shop? A _real_ cake shop?*

Fergus: *I want to be a robber and someone can be a policeman, yeh, yeh. Come on guys, everyone who wants to be a robber come here.*

A group of boys rush to follow him to the role-play area.

I'm making a plan. I'm a robber and I'm stealing an ice cream. I'm going to make a mountain, it's all slippery so no one can catch me. That's the plan.

In the play that followed, all of the boys wanted to be robbers, so one boy who was not a central part of the group was designated to be the policeman. He wandered off and played somewhere else.

Step three: plan ways to develop your space and resources based on your knowledge of boys' interests and preferences

The learning environment that you design will reflect your pedagogy. Discuss your observations as a staff team and share your knowledge of boys' typical development and how children learn best. Ask the children how they think the environment can be improved.

Note any changes that you want to make to the learning environment to:

- ensure that all adults maximise the time spent engaging with boys' and girls' play and tuning into their interests, rather than managing behaviour;
- redesign any under-used learning areas to make them irresistible for all children;
- make sure that there are freely accessible, non-prescriptive resources that provide prompts for challenging and stimulating learning.

These action points help to create an environment that focuses on 'supporting children's in-born intellectual dispositions' (Katz 2015: 2), defined as *the characteristics of effective learning* in the Early Years Foundation Stage (Dowling 2014). 'An appropriate curriculum in the early years . . . is one that includes the encouragement and motivation of children to seek mastery of basic academic skills . . . in the service of their intellectual pursuits' (Katz 2015: 2), empowering children to be effective learners. In an environment where this is achieved successfully, behaviour commonly displayed by boys becomes a positive characteristic that supports creative learning.

Step four: plan ways to develop your space and resources to support boys' personal, social and emotional development, language and fine motor skills

Prime areas are fundamental, work together, and . . . support development in all other areas.

- *Communication and Language*
- *Physical Development and*
- *Personal, Social and Emotional Development.*

(DfE 2014a: 7)

In a safe learning environment where children have a sense of belonging, they can be bold in their learning, while adults help them to explore and discover possibilities and limits. Developmentally, boys can take longer to make secure relationships, develop self-confidence and self-awareness and manage their feelings. They can take longer to develop expressive language and communication skills. They can take longer to develop their fine motor skills. All of these aspects of development are recognised in Early Years curricula globally as being key to children's well-being and fundamental to academic learning. Consider any changes you can make to take into account the need of many boys for enhanced provision in these key areas.

- Use boys' predictable and observed interests as provocations for learning, to show that their interests are valued.
- Use praise and very specific feedback regarding behaviour and learning and helping boys to regulate their behaviour, articulate their feelings and their ideas.
- Promote positive behaviour strategies.
- Provide role models of men in caring roles.
- Encourage boys to emulate role models, such as Olympic athletes, by aiming for their 'PB', their personal best. This introduces the element of competition that many boys love, while every child can feel that they are achieving.
- Create space for boys who like to be active and physical and away from a table by removing some furniture and de-cluttering, as well as making provision for boys who like to be quiet.

- Recognise and provide for boys' need for adventure.

- Provide opportunities for children to practise and develop their expressive language and fine motor skills in active play.

- Reflect on the way that you praise boys and girls. There is some evidence to show that girls are more likely than boys to be praised for being neat, quiet and calm and encouraged to engage in domestic play and static activities, such as puzzles or painting. On the other hand, boys are likely to be praised for thinking independently, being active and encouraged to engage in messy play and rough and tumble games (MacNaughton and Williams 2010).

Step five: consider how you communicate with parents about their son's experiences at home and at school/pre-school

Parents can feel anxious and pressured if their child appears to be struggling to settle into their nursery, pre-school or school. Do your observations of boys and of your environment suggest ways that you can develop your partnership with parents to:

- help parents and children to feel comfortable to share things that they have done at home? For example, by having a display board where children can put up drawings that they have made at home, and where parents can post comments about their child's activities or experiences;

- ensure that parents have a good understanding of the way that their son spends his time? For example, by having a fluid start to the day when parents can stay and read books or do an activity with their child and by displaying photos of the children involved in play and learning.

> In one children's centre, a practitioner brings his dog in and this has proved to be an excellent way to engage with parents and carers, especially men. Staff and parents have casual chats while they pet the dog – sometimes chatting about the children, but also about everyday things. Children love the dog and learn about caring for animals, and they see dads and male carers caring for the dog.

3 Lifting the lid on learning: creating a tinkering workshop

Children reflect back at us the world that we provide for them so we need to make sure that their early experiences are positive ones. Intrinsic motivation is one of the fundamental drivers through which children develop an 'I can' attitude to learning, and different children find intrinsic motivation in different contexts. It is important that we make the environment as full of exciting and flexible opportunities as possible, so that we can capture the varied enthusiasms of all children, boys and girls.

We can do this by turning the classroom into a 'tinkering workshop', a concept that derives from the 'tinkering studio' in the Exploratorium, a San Francisco museum (http://tinkering.exploratorium.edu).

What does a 'tinkering workshop' look like?

Any sufficiently advanced form of learning is indistinguishable from play.
(Scott Snibbe, seen in the Exploratorium in San Francisco)

The creators of the tinkering studio describe it as a 'workshop for playful invention, investigation and collaboration' where learning is 'immersive . . . active . . . and curiosity-driven' and where people can 'become deeply engaged in an investigation . . . explore . . . create' (http://tinkering.exploratorium.edu/about). This echoes the belief that well-being and involvement are essential to deep-level learning (Laevers 2005). In a 'tinkering workshop', boys and girls can make and create things that have a genuine purpose for them, testing out hypotheses as they meet a challenge or potential obstacle, discovering that learning comes through taking risks and making mistakes. This approach builds on children's innate learning strategies, allowing them to be confident and active learners – physically and cognitively.

How can we create a tinkering workshop?

1 Create provocations for learning that inspire boys

That's an ankylosaurus, he smashes people with his tail.

Children can become explorers and scientists, engineers, artists and philosophers, in a workshop where adults provide provocations or prompts for learning and children have the space and time to 'tinker' with ideas and resources. The best way to capture the interest of any child is to observe the play and identify suitable provocations that can extend children's learning. Provocations that particularly inspire boys can be:

- real-life activities, such as gardening, cooking or putting up shelves;
- predictable interests, such as dragons, witches and wizards, pirates and space travel, which are almost guaranteed to be good starting points for learning.

A practitioner created some packs with writing frames that supported children's predictable interests, which she could bring out as and when they were needed.

In an environment where children are asked, 'What do you want to find out?' rather than being instructed and tested on what they know (Katz 2015), they can continue to be reflective learners. The key is to be prepared: with ideas and resources that can supplement, but not dominate, children's play, and then be on hand to listen to their questions and help them to explore possibilities. Children can be encouraged to share their ideas and their discoveries with other children, with staff and with parents.

Children in a reception class are all asked what they would like to learn about at the beginning of term. Parents are asked if they have any specialist knowledge and those that do are invited to support children in their investigations. When the children are ready, they lead workshops for other children, sharing their new discoveries, skills and knowledge. Together the children, parents and practitioners become teachers and learners.

Children asked to learn about:

- electricity – what it is and how it works;
- how snow falls;
- what toast is made of and how it gets to toast;
- why horses have sharp teeth;
- how to drive a train.

2 Provide extended time for learning

If it goes right the first time you're just learning to follow instructions.

(http://www.tinkeringschool.com/our-philosophy/)

In a tinkering workshop, children are seen as competent learners who are willing and able to try things, accept setbacks, and take pride in their personal achievements. When children's thinking is taken seriously, they can tackle and express complex ideas, as Charlie, age 3.10, shows us:

Charlie puts on his special explorer hat and packs his rucksack so that he can be a dinosaur explorer, imitating a character on a television programme. He notices his dad watching him.

Charlie: *I've got a hypothesis.*

Charlie's
father: *Have you? What's a hypothesis?*

Charlie: *It's an idea that you can check out.*

Children are like sponges, soaking up the positive and negative experiences that they encounter. Given the right opportunities, they can surprise us with their ability to understand and use words such as 'hypothesis'. Charlie has been watching a television programme about dinosaur discoveries. He has spent so much time playing dinosaurs that, in the right context – one that has meaning for the child – the new word could be absorbed alongside the familiar and used appropriately. In Early Years settings, we need to minimise the time that children spend sitting and waiting, for example at whole class registration, and maximise the time they spend tinkering with interesting materials to see what they can discover.

3 Provide inclusive resources for learning

There must be a wheel gene on the Y chromosome!

(Eliot 2012: 106)

In a tinkering workshop boys and girls explore genuine challenges and are trusted to use real tools and real materials such as wood, nails, rope, wheels and bricks.

Gender-specific styles of play have been shown to be similar in very different cultures, suggesting that there is something innate in the way that boys and girls choose toys, from as early as a child's first birthday. While it is important that we acknowledge and respect children's choice of toys, we also need to question and challenge the way that we present certain toys and resources to avoid limiting children's options or placing negative value on certain types of play. 'In childhood, toys become part of a playful process of becoming oneself' (Holman 2016). We are in danger of restricting boys' and girls' sense of self if we fail to provide play options that challenge stereotypical play.

Observations of boys and girls show that, while girls might choose to play with some traditionally 'boys' toys', such as construction, wheeled vehicles and action figures, boys are much less likely to choose to play with traditionally 'girls' toys' such as dolls and they commonly make negative responses to suggestions that they play with these toys ('No way', 'Yuk, that's girlie'). This difference relates to issues of power and status that persist into adulthood. While women are breaking into spheres of work that have been male-dominated, traditionally female jobs such as nursing or childcare still attract lower pay and status. Parents' attitudes, in particular the attitudes of fathers, are likely to be influenced, however unconsciously, by concerns that their son will lose status if he plays with 'girls' toys', as this might lead him into a lower-status role as an adult. Sometimes these messages are expressed directly, as in the case below, but children pick the messages up even when they are unconsciously transmitted.

> **Context:** the beginning of a session in a pre-school.
> Mark runs in and immediately goes to the home corner and puts on a wedding dress and high-heeled shoes. His Dad tells him sharply to 'take them off!'

Some things to consider when resourcing a tinkering workshop:

- Provide resources that aren't gender-stereotypical, to give children wide options.
- Provide resources that reflect the things that boys and girls value.
- Avoid making implicit and explicit judgements about the toys that children choose to play with, while encouraging children to question the judgements that they make about toys for boys and toys for girls.
- Observe where boys choose to go and put resources that they don't choose to use into active play.
- Reflect all children's interests, experiences and family cultures.
- Assess risk benefits. Set boundaries and expectations so that children can use wood-work tools, sticks and other potentially dangerous objects safely.
- Provide open-ended resources, also known as 'loose parts': materials that can be used creatively and non-prescriptively. Loose parts help children to develop their initiative, imagination, creativity and technical skills. Large loose parts require col-laborative effort to move and balance. Children can develop fine motor skills when they use small loose parts. Sharing ideas and challenges help children to develop their language for thinking and descriptive and narrative language, while tidying away loose parts requires children to develop a sense of social responsibility.
- Ensure that resources are constantly accessible to allow children to revisit the same play.

Loose parts can be large, such as planks, pallets or crates, or small, such as balls, shells, gravel or twigs. They can extend play by becoming a house or a vehicle, or a phone, or a magic potion: anything that allows the play to develop. Loose parts can be combined in different ways to develop children's problem-solving and technical skills, adding wheels to a model to make a vehicle or balancing a roof on a model building, attaching material to a pole to make a den, or adding a fuel tank to a model rocket . . .

4 Provide adult models, challenge and encouragement

Tahir climbs onto a wobbly structure that he has made from four hollow blocks in his reception class outside area. A teacher walks past and tells him to be careful. She stops and says cheerfully: *You're taller than me now! Are you taller or smaller than me?*

Tahir jumps down. He ignores her caution and her question as he is concentrating on making his tower more stable. When he's satisfied with the stability of the tower, he climbs up and raises his arms triumphantly.

What is the role of the adult in a tinkering workshop? Research has shown that boys respond well to interventions from older boys or men, who tend to interact through 'casual mentoring' (Jarvis, in Broadhead et al. 2010: 71), for example, joining in with a football game, modelling skills and language, while female intervention can be didactic or supervisory. In Tahir's case, there was a danger that his learning would be closed down but he carried on with the task in hand and ignored the teacher's intervention. This benefited his learning, but could have caused problems for him if his behaviour had been seen as insolent or uncooperative.

As children experiment, they learn that things might not turn out as planned and, in a tinkering workshop, this can open up exciting possibilities. Children and adults become co-constructors of knowledge, as adults provide 'achievable challenge with appropriate assistance' (Whitebread, in Broadhead et al. 2010: 173) and model *learning*, not *knowing*. In this way, children can develop the dispositions to learn from their mistakes and failures, persisting when they meet serious challenges.

Tricia is a reception / year 1 teacher in an inner city school. She adapted her classroom and timetable to increase the time children could spend in child-initiated learning, creating space by taking some tables out of the classroom, providing stimulating open-ended resources and minimising the time children spent in formal, adult-led, table-based learning:

It's the children's classroom now, they really have a sense of ownership. They don't want to go out to play, they'd rather carry on with their play in the classroom! Behaviour has improved because the children are always busy.

In a tinkering workshop, children will be able to develop positive learning dispositions, self-confidence, self-regulation, social skills, language skills and fine motor skills. These areas of development are crucial for all children and they are all areas where boys often need additional support. The following strategies can help practitioners to provide this support:

- *Model the language of thinking*, questioning, wondering and planning.
- *Model and encourage children's cooperative play and collaborative learning*.
- *Talk about risks and strategies to minimise risk* rather than banning activities.
- *Support children to develop their ability to self-regulate* by using props such as timers that help children to wait for their turn without getting frustrated. Give instructions in terms that children can understand, rather than simply asserting authority.

> At the end of the nursery session, the nursery teacher needed the children to come in from the garden. As he walked past the sandpit, he called out: *Hey guys, the beach is closing*, rather than telling the children that it was time to come out of the sandpit.

- *Establish clear and consistent routines and provide cues for transitions*: transition times can be difficult times for boys who have less well-developed language skills and impulse control. Create 'markers' for routines and transitions, such as a visual timetable, musical cues or physical signals, such as raising a flag in the garden as a cue to tidy up. These non-verbal markers also help children learning English as an additional language.
- *Trust children and give them responsibility in their learning*: give children choices in their play and support their fascinations by providing appropriate resources and by learning alongside them.
- *Trust children and give them responsibility in the learning environment*: children can be given specific jobs, for example, tidying up the sand toys. Label accessible resources with words and pictures to encourage independence.

Conclusion

> Building on each gender's strengths, adults can shape the environment to better round out children's development, giving both boys and girls the tinge of purple that will help them be happier and more successful.
>
> (Eliot 2010: 105)

In this chapter, we considered the value of stepping back and observing children so that we can create an appropriate learning environment – a tinkering workshop – where children can explore and express their curiosity about the world. In the following chapters, we look in detail at suitable provision that supports boys and girls to express themselves creatively as they become confident movers, articulate talkers, sensitive listeners and confident problem-solvers, while developing formal academic skills.

Summary

- Children learn best when they have high levels of well-being and involvement (Laevers 2005).

- Observe boys to determine their levels of well-being and involvement.

- Evaluate your provision and make changes to resources, adult support and space that will improve boys' levels of well-being and involvement.

- Create a tinkering workshop that supports boys' holistic development and active learning styles – and girls benefit too.

- Provide provocations for learning, establish boundaries and expectations, and then give children freedom to learn.

5 Becoming a confident mover

Introduction

Dylan, age 6, is out for a walk in the woods with his grandparents. He runs ahead along a narrow path, making regular detours to slide down a muddy slope or to duck into bushes at the side of the path. Every few yards he picks up a stick or a stone and throws it into the trees, yelling: *TNT, yeh! It's the best!* or he creates a machine gun out of a fallen branch, making explosive sounds.

When they get to a shallow stream at the bottom of the hill, he steps confidently onto the rocks in the water where he crouches down, motionless, and peers into the water, looking for tiny fish. His concentration is complete. After some minutes, he lifts up one foot, picks up the stone that his foot had been resting on, and he places it in the water nearby. Then he steps carefully across to where he has placed the stone, shifting his balance from one leg to two again, and he continues his search for fish. Gradually he moves around the stream, crouching

(continued)

(continued)

down with perfect confidence and balance, spotting fish and trying to catch them in his hands, until he stands up triumphantly, to show his grandparents the tiny fish that he is holding gently in his palms. As soon as his grandparents have seen the fish, he puts it back into the stream.

Dylan was in his element on the way down to the stream, when he was active and noisy, throwing things, shouting and pretending to fight. Like many boys of all ages, Dylan loves action, power struggles, challenges and adventure. He was also in his element when he was being quiet, focused and still. He reminds us that boys can be active, but they can also be thoughtful, focused and caring. We can strengthen all of boys' capabilities by providing a learning environment that inspires boys by reflecting their fascinations and learning styles.

In this chapter, we consider how we can extend the learning environment for boys and for girls, and give all children time, space and opportunities to be active, adventurous and to seek out genuine challenges. We explore ways to provide continuous provision that allows boys and girls to be active learners without reinforcing gender stereotypes. We look at some boy-friendly, enticing and irresistible activities and resources that encourage boys to develop the fine motor skills that they need to record, present and develop their ideas and thinking: fine motor skills that typically develop earlier in girls than boys.

1 Evaluating the environment to support boys' learning styles

Children are natural explorers and discoverers, and they show us how they learn when we watch them play in an open and stimulating learning environment. It is important that we listen to children and use their interests to give meaning to their learning. Deep-level learning takes place when children display high involvement levels (Laevers 2005). 'Involvement goes along with a strong feeling of satisfaction stemming from the exploratory drive, which makes the activity intrinsically motivating' (Directorate for Education and Skills, OECD 2004: 6).

We can create an environment that promotes intrinsic motivation in the following ways:

- Observe and support children's play outside and inside: where do children choose to go? Who do they play with? What type of play do they choose?

  Do adults support play and learning in the places where boys choose to go? Can boys access stimulating resources in the areas where they choose to play? How are resources and opportunities for learning planned, to extend boys' play and learning in these areas?

- Evaluate children's levels of well-being and involvement (Laevers 2005).

Are boys' levels of well-being and involvement higher in some areas of the learning environment than others? Can we provide resources and opportunities in all areas of learning that extend boys' experiences?

- Evaluate the level of physical and cognitive challenge in children's play: are children limiting themselves to the same type of play or are they willing to try new things, take sensible risks and experiment with new ideas and experiences?

How do adults provide resources and opportunities that challenge and extend boys' knowledge, skills and thinking?

- Evaluate the degree to which children are developing positive learning dispositions: are they curious and willing to explore the world around them?

Are boys supported to decide on their own goals, plan ways to reach these goals, persist when they meet a challenge and show satisfaction when they achieve something that they set out to do?

Our observations can help us to extend the learning territory, physically and intellectually, to give children a sense of exciting possibilities. This can happen inside or outside, but many indoor resources are designed with a specific purpose that directs learning in a particular way. Children need some specific learning resources, but they also need outdoor spaces that can provide limitless possibilities, where they have greater freedom to be active and creative, to develop critical thinking skills and teamwork: genuine life skills which can diminish if they aren't given the chance to flourish.

2 Why do children need to move?

Young children learn holistically and their physical, social, language and communication, and cognitive development are all interdependent. All aspects of children's development can come together in an environment that provides opportunities for play and exploratory learning.

Developing physical control and fine and gross motor skills

> motor skills at different stages of development provide a reflection of maturity in the functioning of the central nervous system – the relationship between the brain and body – which provides the foundations for learning.
>
> (Goddard Blythe 2011: 131)

When we watch boys play, we often see them using oodles of physical energy! Physical play is an essential part of childhood for boys and girls and an enabling learning environment is one that harnesses boys' physical energy and also gives girls the chance to be active and adventurous.

Physical play supports large muscle development and allows children to develop gross motor skills naturally as they run and walk, hop and skip, jump and climb, throw and catch.

It is through their physical play that children develop small muscle strength and control as they fill a bucket with soil or sand, hammer nails into wood at the woodwork bench and build constructions using a variety of techniques.

Gross and fine motor skills improve as a result of children's experiences. They develop side by side as children need core strength and stability before they develop dexterity with their limbs and hands. Children develop strength, agility, balance and coordination, muscle tone and stability in their trunk through active play, and once this strong, solid base is established, the arm and hand are free to make the precise, coordinated movements needed for drawing, cutting and writing.

Boys typically develop gross motor skills in advance of girls, and fine motor skills develop later in boys than girls, as we saw in Chapter 2. This can influence judgements that Early Years practitioners make about children. Boys typically choose to exercise their gross motor skills by being on the move, away from adults, while girls are more likely to be found at sedentary adult-planned activities. It is very important that we recognise that children's fine motor skills and the ability to sit still are not an indication of children's intelligence: they simply allow children to present their work neatly and confidently. We need to be wary of allowing girls' greater fine motor skills to set up higher (and often self-fulfilling) expectations, while creating lower expectations for boys.

We can raise our expectations for boys by observing them in their active, physical and purposeful play, where they can demonstrate their competencies.

Developing language and communication skills

Physical play can allow children to develop their language and communication skills. They learn to establish rules in their active play, to set boundaries and resolve conflicts. They can play imaginatively and constructively with other children, strengthening social bonds and learning how to listen to others and work as a team.

As with fine motor skills, language skills typically develop more slowly in boys than in girls (Eliot 2012), but they are ultimately dependent on experience. We can give boys enhanced experiences to help them develop their language and communication skills through the provision of high-quality physical play. In Chapter 6 we explore ways to do this.

Supporting cognitive development

Physical play supports all areas of cognitive learning. It is through their physical play that children develop an understanding of mathematical and scientific concepts as they throw or roll or push things and learn how different objects (and their own bodies) move through space, at different velocities, forming different trajectories depending on their size, shape and weight. They learn about rhythm and patterns as they hop, jump and twirl. They become familiar with plants and living creatures, they learn about the seasons and how the physical environment changes through the year, in rain and wind, sun, frost and snow as they play outside. In Chapters 7 and 8 we explore appropriate environments where children can develop their problem-solving skills and understanding of the world.

3 Planning the physical environment to support active learning

A large-scale longitudinal study that investigated the aspects of provision that contribute to quality in Early Years settings (Sylva et al. 2004) used a rating scale called ECERS-R to evaluate learning environments. Findings showed that children in centres with lower ECERS-R scores spent shorter periods of time in active behaviour and learning, while loose parts and open-ended resources prompted more active play and learning.

We can help our boys to get 'up and running' in their learning by developing our understanding of the way in which different spaces trigger different types of behaviour, play and learning. The way that the physical space is planned and set up, inside and outside, will reflect the pedagogy of the setting and the expectations that adults have of children.

An enabling environment provides options for different types of play and learning: areas for planned learning, based on practitioners' knowledge of the specific learning objectives that they want to cover; areas that suggest a certain type of play and learning, but that have less prescriptive learning objectives; and open and flexible spaces where children can choose the resources and how they play.

Developing the outside area

Outdoor spaces need physical boundaries to keep children safe while allowing for appropriate risk-taking that will challenge adventurous and more timid children. The outside area can feel noisy and chaotic to less confident children. Physical boundaries and defined spaces can help to break up a large area, for instance using bushes, tyres or logs to create separate areas for ball games, bike riding, rough and tumble play, quiet play, and an area for less mobile children. Outside areas should have:

- spaces and places that offer physical challenge, such as trees with low branches, a climbing frame with a ladder, rope netting, monkey bars and a fireman's pole;
- natural landscapes and different surfaces that change over the seasons: grass and mud, sand that can be wet or dry, tarmac that can be dry or full of puddles, cobbles that can become slippery. Children learn to push their personal boundaries as they navigate uneven terrain, developing confidence and self-control;

- shaded areas for summer sun and shelter from rain and wind. Children can explore the outside in all weathers if they have suitable clothing for all seasons, such as sun hats and woolly hats and warm all-in-one waterproofs;

- a large sand pit, where several children can play and work together;

- independent access to water, through an outside tap or water butt;

- a digging area – just for digging!

- a gardening area, for growing vegetables and wild and cultivated flowers, to develop an interest in nature and botany;

- climbing areas, ideally with moveable equipment that can be turned into a train, a pirate ship or a circus arena. Minimise the amount of fixed equipment that will have fewer uses.

Developing the inside area

The inside area, like the outdoor area, should be set up to encourage children to explore and find out, not to check what they know (Katz 2015). Children need to be able to 'flow' between areas and carry resources between the inside and outside, to make connections in their learning:

- Move quiet areas close together and make sufficient space for large, physical activity such as large block play. Put linked resources close together, such as small blocks and small world.

- Monitor provision to see how the boys and girls use different spaces, and make sure that no group dominates certain areas.

- Minimise the number of tables, to allow children to move freely, and replace some tables with floor mats. Boys often prefer to play and work on the floor, stretched out or standing or leaning on a surface, ready to move.

- Put familiar resources in unexpected places, for example put sand on a tarpaulin on the floor inside for a change.

- Provide spaces where boys can express themselves physically and to encourage girls to be active on the few days when you can't get outside.

Inside and outside

- Create enticing hideaway spaces where a child can go with one or two friends to encourage secret play, talk and interaction, book sharing or daydreaming!

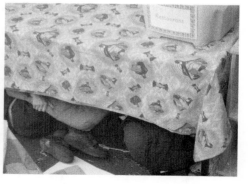

Attractive and snug spaces . . . and children will make their own hideaways under tables!

- Set up a rough and tumble or 'rough housing' area with mats or soft play areas inside or outside.

Rough and tumble play often emerges when boys start to play in groups (Eliot 2012: 123–30). Adult reactions in group settings can be negative, especially among women, who, studies show, worry more than men about the dangers, disruption and noise associated with this type of play (Carr 2001). However, this can have a damaging effect on the relationships between female practitioners and boys, and on boys' ability to manage their aggressive behaviour, if value judgements are made about boys' behaviour without recognising the benefits of this type of play.

The benefits of rough and tumble play, or 'rough housing' (Maccoby, in Baron-Cohen 2004) are well researched and documented. Rough and tumble play activates different parts of the brain, as well as the body: the amygdalae, which processes emotions; the cerebellum, which handles complex motor skills; and the prefrontal cortex, which makes high-level judgements (Panksepp 2004). It helps children bond, set boundaries, deal with aggression and resolve conflicts.

A school in Iceland has a small soft play room where children can choose to go and shut the door. The room has been designed to be safe: it has a carpet and only has soft play equipment. The door has a high window so that the children have a sense of privacy when the door is shut – it is like a soft play den – but the adults can monitor the play discreetly from the outside.

The balance between the environment and learning and teaching is subtle and requires sensitive planning and sensitivity in adult responses to situations as they arise. The play and learning in the scenario below is possible because the environment gives the children resources that they can use creatively (the crates and planks), resources that promote specific learning (the clipboards and paper) and a practitioner who understands how to extend play without disrupting it.

Luke, Albert and Rajinder are playing pirates in their reception class garden. They have built a pirate ship out of crates and planks next to the sand pit and are energetically climbing to the top of the ship and jumping down, yelling. Their teacher, William, walks past and calls out: *Land ahoy, Cap'n, I spy a treasure island!* and he places a box of clipboards and paper down next to the ship. Albert climbs to the top of the ship to look through a pair of binoculars to see if he can spot the treasure island. He squeals excitedly: *Aaargh, I can see it, look out!* He calls Rajinder and Luke over and whispers to them, suggesting they make a treasure map for their teacher. They take a clipboard and huddle in the playhouse out of sight to make their secret map, which they show delightedly to their teacher.

In the following section, we consider the types of resources that we can provide to engage boys in active learning.

4 Resources to promote fine and gross motor skills

Loose parts

A group of children were playing side by side in the mud kitchen in their pre-school:

Mac: *I'm making drinking chocolate.*

Betty: *I'm making cement.*

Alexis: *It's got leaves and stones.*

Loose parts and open-ended resources invite children to play in their own individual way, exploring their fascinations, developing their imagination and developing practical skills as they explore and make sense of the world around them through their play. Loose parts place no restrictions on children's imaginations, as we see in the observation of children playing in a mud kitchen, where each child responds to the mud kitchen in their own way. Children can focus on the process of learning, rather than trying to achieve an end product that has been predetermined by an adult. This style of play suits many boys and benefits all children. It is highly inclusive as every child can play at their own level together with other children.

When loose parts are available in the continuous provision, learning can happen in contexts that are fun, challenging and purposeful.

Supporting children's physical play

Small loose parts, such as shells, gravel or twigs, support the development of fine motor skills: for example, pegging material, tying rope, lashing canes together with twine, attaching material, picking up small sticks and pebbles or hammering. Large loose parts, such as planks, pallets or crates, tyres, bricks, crates, or logs, support the development of gross motor skills in large open spaces: for example, rolling, lifting, positioning, pushing and pulling.

Supporting children's language and communication skills

Children can play with loose parts collaboratively: negotiating and setting rules that allow them to function safely and fairly in a group.

> Xander is trying to work out how he can lift a heavy plank onto an A-frame to make a ramp into his 'pirate ship'. He calls Joss over and asks him to take one end and he takes the other end. Together, they lift the plank and place it where they want it to go.

Supporting children's cognitive skills

Loose parts support active play, cognitively as well as physically. They can be moved around and combined in different ways to develop children's problem-solving, visual-spatial skills and technical skills. A tyre can become a wheel for a train, a seat with a cushion inside it, a table with a cloth over it, or a planter with earth inside.

When children play with loose parts, they can set their own challenges and test their own limits, explore, experiment, hypothesise and adapt their thinking (DfE 2014).

> Sam is 3 and is playing at home with his cars. His mother gets out some recycled food boxes and pieces of card that she has taken from cereal boxes.
>
> Sam creates a road layout on the floor from the card, and makes a bus depot for his new and very special toy bus. He tells his mother that the bus depot has sleeping rooms for the bus drivers, a bus wash, a bay where the buses can dry off, and a car park on the roof, with a petrol pump. He adds a cinema and a hospital with a helipad so that sick people can be flown in.

(continued)

(continued)

Gathering loose parts: what do they look like?

Loose parts are gender-neutral, although the language used by adults can inadvertently encourage gender-stereotypical play: for example, by making implicit assumptions that boys are more interested in building, while thinking that girls might prefer to 'cook' in the mud kitchen. It is important that we avoid making value judgements about stereotypical boys' and girls' play when we see it happening, but we can discuss and challenge stereotypes with the children.

Loose parts can include:

- natural resources that children can find outside, such as stones, twigs, leaves, seeds and gravel, logs, bark chippings;
- 'real stuff', such as ropes, nails, wooden offcuts, bricks, straw, sticks, and bamboo canes;
- recycled materials – fabric, cardboard boxes and tubes, plastic containers, bottle and jar lids;
- equipment that has flexible uses – balls, buckets, rope, crates, guttering, transparent tubing or guttering with coloured liquids, baskets, pallets, pegs, tables, tyres, tarpaulin, tubes, old chairs without legs, plastic pipes, nets (for dens or trapping baddies!), steering wheels;
- small loose parts, such as buttons, sequins, feathers, bottle tops and corks.

5 Some activities to encourage fine and gross motor development

Boys' predictable interests can be used to set up activities, which encourage them to develop their fine and gross motor skills. Girls will also have fun with these activities!

- Create a car wash, wash the wheels (using a circular movement) and windows (using a vertical movement) with sponges and brushes.

  Ask the children for ideas for other kinds of vehicle washes: a super-hero vehicle wash, a bike wash, a carriage wash (for Cinderella and the Prince), a rocket wash.

- Set up den-building opportunities that involve children in gross motor movements, such as lifting, pushing and rolling, and fine motor skills when they tie, thread or fasten string and pegs.

- Prepare and cook food, stirring and spooning cake mixture, cutting and spreading fillings for sandwiches, peeling and chopping fruit. Use real food or 'cook' in a mud kitchen.

  Make food for a giant, for pirates, aliens and superheroes, adventurers and explorers, trolls and space travellers.

- Add an element of competition into fine motor activities to entice the boys: time how quickly can you pick up worms with tweezers or dangerous creatures such as snakes with long-handled tongs (use the plastic variety of creatures, not real ones!).

- Mix your own play dough, to strengthen small hands, adding different colours, textures and smells to the mixture.

- Create a 'make and mend' station. Children can develop fine motor dexterity when they take apart equipment such as old radios or computer keyboards using a screwdriver, spanner and wire cutters. They can build their own creations at a woodwork bench using a hammer and saw and nails.

- Sing action rhymes that involve coordinated finger actions.

- Create trails using objects such as pebbles and twigs (picking up small objects and placing them precisely develops the movement required to hold a pencil), or a liquid trail using washing up liquid bottles or small sprays (developing finger and hand strength through pressing and squeezing).

- Set up a fine motor 'tinkering station' with beads, sequins, corks, string and other small objects displayed in attractive containers of different shapes, sizes and materials, such as egg trays, ice cube trays or wicker baskets.

- Develop different areas outside linked to a superhero or space travel theme (this can be adapted for other predictable interests, such as pirates or explorers). Make speed limit signs; traffic rules; landing strips and arrivals and departure areas from different planets; space vehicle parking bays and a mechanics' bay; a service station for refreshments and naps; a shop to buy equipment for a journey.

- Reproduce similar ideas on a small scale using small world resources, with homemade maps.

6 Some practicalities and management issues

Extending boundaries in the learning environment can require a shift in the balance between planned and responsive learning and teaching, which might feel quite daunting for practitioners who feel most comfortable with a definite plan for the day! In Reggio Emilia, a well-planned, stimulating environment is described as a 'third teacher', which offers children time and space to take the initiative in their learning. This can change the role of the adults from 'covering the curriculum' to helping children to 'uncover' the learning. Boys' play often demonstrates their need to set challenges for themselves and push their personal boundaries, and they thrive when they are given the space, resources and opportunities for active learning that we have explored in this chapter (Cigman 2014, Solly 2015, Tovey, in Broadhead et al. 2010).

Risk and adventure

We need to make sure that children can explore safely, but this doesn't mean creating a risk-averse environment, by eradicating any challenge, as we saw in Chapter 4. We can facilitate physical and challenging play by scaffolding children's experiences, stepping up the challenge in an activity gradually, to build up children's confidence. We can help children learn strategies to keep themselves safe.

An Early Years setting in Iceland for children aged 2 to 6 years

Children have extended time outside every day wearing warm, padded, all-in-one suits in cold weather.

Children of all ages were observed climbing and running down wet and slippery slopes with excellent balance and control. A 2-year-old child fell over as she came down a slope. She deliberately fell onto her forearms with her palms facing up, protecting her hands and protected by her padded arms. Other children lay on the slope and in the sand having some 'downtime', alone or with other children.

Children showed good balance and coordination, confidence and independence.

- Agree ground rules for using potentially hazardous equipment. The number of children using a woodwork bench will need to be limited, and certain rules established about the use of tools, for example, wood can only be sawed when it is in a vice, children can be shown how to hold a nail when they are hammering and how to use a hand drill safely.

- Take photos of different risks and talk about them with the children, for example have photographs of suitable and unsuitable clothing for wearing outside when children are climbing.

- Talk to the children about what they would like to have in the inside and outside areas. Discuss ways of putting their ideas into practice safely and in a way that suits all of the children, and help children to think about how they can take some responsibility for their own safety.

In a school in Iceland, practitioners became concerned when children started to climb onto the roof of the playhouse outside (it was about 2 metres high). They considered banning this, but they watched carefully, and discovered that older, more confident children were looking out for less confident climbers and helping them to climb safely. Staff talked with the children and they all agreed a rule that children could climb onto the roof if they could get up themselves.

- Boys can take up more space than girls, so set up systems to make this fair, sometimes limiting the places and spaces where boys can go.

- Break up long straight spaces or circular tracks that encourage children to charge around. Turn a straight space into a role-play runway or landing strip to encourage a specific focus in boys' play. Add cones, chalk marks or other obstacles on the ground to a circular track to encourage varied movement. Make stop signs and traffic signs to control the flow/speed. Set up 'traffic police' with clipboards to write reports.

- Make sure that there are enough adults to be in different areas, with some adults who can support learning, not just 'police' an area.

- Have male and female role models who support active and quiet play, reading books and engaging in rough housing with boys and girls.

- Have spare clothes / waterproof suits (for adults and children!) so that parents don't worry about active and messy play.

7 Sharing benefits of active play with parents (and all staff)

Research by Morrongiello (in Eliot 2012: 135) suggests that parents perceive risk-taking differently depending on if their child is a boy or girl. This research found that when daughters' play involved risky behaviour, the parents focused on safety, but when their sons took similar risks, the parents focused on discipline rather than safety. Other research studies have shown that parents have higher expectations of their sons' physical capabilities than of their daughters' abilities (Eliot 2012: 64).

This suggests that parents' (and quite probably, practitioners') attitudes are influencing how well children develop physical skills and confidence. Girls and boys have a right to equal access to risky activities, so it is important that we share the benefits of active, physical play with parents, while reassuring them that proper risk assessments have been done and serious risks have been eliminated. This can be done informally, through conversations with parents, and at a parents' meeting, where examples of children's learning through physical play can be shared. Important messages can also be shared through displays of photographs of children involved in challenging and exciting play, with explanations of curriculum learning and children's own words in speech bubbles.

Conclusion

One school in New Zealand that promoted the value of outdoor adventurous spaces and play in their school found that giving the children *space, time, trust* and *loose parts* increased children's confidence and coordination and improved children's ability to concentrate in the classroom (Strauss 2015).

In this chapter, we have explored ways to extend the experiences that children have for active and physical play in order to enhance their learning. In the following chapter, we consider how active play can support boys' language and communication skills.

Summary

- Physically active learning supports children's gross and fine motor development, language and communications skills, and cognitive development as well as their health and well-being.

- Extend the learning territory, physically and intellectually, by observing where boys choose to go and enhancing experiences for active and adventurous learning as well as for quiet and still experiences.

- Provide open-ended resources, inside and outside, that support all aspects of children's learning and development.

- Establish the risk benefits of physical and challenging play, as well as minimising any serious risk.

- Support parents to value and promote physically active play.

Becoming a confident communicator

Introduction

> Rory, age 2½, is having breakfast with his Dad.
>
> Dad: *A chicken laid this egg for your breakfast.*
>
> Rory pauses and thinks, then asks: *Who did lay the Weetabix for our breakfast?*

Rory is in an early stage of his journey as a language learner, but already he is able to listen carefully and respond as part of a turn-taking conversation. He is also able to use language to explore ideas, make sense of the world, ask for information and make connections between his experience and new learning. In this chapter, we explore how young children become active communicators. We consider how we can mitigate the slight disadvantage that boys have in their language development. We see how adults can provide a language-rich environment and support for all boys and girls that will allow them to become confident talkers and learners, and active members of their social groups.

1 Acquiring early language skills

Young children have an extraordinary capacity to develop language from birth, without any kind of formal teaching. They learn:

- **Phonology:** how to use the sound system of their language. In monolingual children, this develops from about the sixth month onwards, when babies start to form the sounds of their home language(s) and lose the ability to articulate the sounds of other languages.

- **Semantics:** understanding words and developing a wide vocabulary. Children learn to make sense of language in a way that goes beyond the literal meaning of the words: 'The whole room got up and left.'

- **Syntax:** developing longer and more complex sentences to enhance self-expression. Children absorb and apply the grammatical rules of their home language in regular and irregular forms: 'I goed to the park' becomes 'I did go to the park today' before a child learns the irregular 'I went . . .'.

- **Pragmatics:** understanding the conventions that relate to ways of communicating within a language. Children learn appropriate ways of communicating in different contexts.

Gender influences in language development

> Whereas language ability is only subtly affected by a child's gender, it is strongly affected by his or her environment.
>
> (Eliot 2012: 70)

We saw in Chapter 2 that language skills generally develop earlier in girls than in boys. During infancy, babies develop the ability to communicate through 'proto-conversations' (Trevarthen 2013), using eye contact, gestures and sounds to interact (and turning away when they have had enough of a conversation!). At the same time, they develop their understanding of language (receptive language) and, typically, a nine-month-old girl and a ten-month-old boy will understand about fifty words. By the age of twenty-two months, typically, girls have an expressive language bank of about three hundred different words, while boys reach this stage by about twenty-three or twenty-four months (Eliot 2012: 70).

In all aspects of child development, there is a normal range within which children reach their developmental milestones. With regard to language, gender differences are real but slight, perhaps influenced by postnatal testosterone in boys, which slows down brain development, resulting in slower maturation of language processing abilities – although research is not conclusive (Eliot 2012: 90). In consequence, 'Girls tend to be on the earlier end, and boys on the later end, of this age range', according to researchers Seyda Özçalskan and Susan Goldin-Meadow (cited in Lowry 2010).

Although there are some developmental differences between boys and girls, it's clear that language skills are highly influenced by the amount of exposure that babies and young children have to language and positive interactions. The environment that children experience is crucial, especially at a time of rapid brain growth in the first few years. Parents and Early Years practitioners have a powerful role to play in countering any biological differences that impact on language development.

Social communicators

Young children learn to talk in everyday, meaningful contexts, absorbing and using the mechanics and pragmatics of language from the people around them (Vygotsky 1978) when they are intrinsically motivated to communicate and interact. Babies seek out companionship with their carers from birth, actively initiating communicative episodes. This capacity to communicate will thrive if it is reinforced through 'imaginative companionship': reciprocal, responsive interactions by a caring adult that help to establish an emotional attachment and support early language development. A child who meets with positive responses will become a '"linguistic genius", eager to tell stories, sometimes matching the language of parents and siblings, sometimes inventing words' (Trevarthen 2013).

Children 'actively construct their language using a combination of their experience and their innate language-making capacity' (The Conversation 2016). Children learn from people around them, absorbing the structure of the language as well as the vocabulary. But they also use language that they haven't heard, intelligently applying linguistic rules to irregular words in the language, for example, 'I maked a rocket', and they can be creative in the ways that they apply their developing knowledge, making it fit their understanding of the world.

> Simon, age 3, is crying and holding his ear in pain: *I've got a dire ear, I've got a dire ear.* Simon has heard the word diarrhoea, but hasn't understood its meaning. He inventively attributes a meaning to the word that matches his experience.

Children's language is learnt within the culture of the society in which they live (Vygotsky, in Rose and Rogers 2012: 51) and it is a tool that they can use to play an increasingly active part in society. Children's developing language skills contribute to their social integration and their capacity to learn and be creative.

Language for learning

The child's intellectual growth is contingent on his mastering the social means of thought, that is, language.

(Vygotsky, quoted in Whitehead 1997: 62)

When children first start to use expressive language, they use what Piaget called 'ego-centric' speech, and Vygotsky called 'private speech': a monologue or running commentary during their play, or in their cot when they wake up. Initially, their language is concrete, about things that are visible or of immediate significance.

As children internalise language, 'private speech' becomes 'inner speech' (Vygotsky 1987), the internal monologue that we have running inside our heads as adults. Language becomes a transformative tool by giving us the capacity for symbolic thought that frees us 'from the constraints of the physically and temporally present, the here and now' and allows us to 'create totally new worlds of the mind and the imagination' (Whitehead 1997: 61). Even the simplest first words, labels such as *cup* or *dog,* make intellectual demands on the child, requiring them to identify differences between a cup and a bowl or a glass, and recognise similarities between a big, white dog such as a husky and a small, brown dog such as a dachshund: early stages in scientific classification. By the age of 2, a child can understand the difference between 'my mummy' and 'a mummy', moving from the personal to the universal.

2 What shall we talk about?

As children develop their receptive and expressive language skills, they get better at making sense of their growing experience of the world. Rory, by the age of 3, no longer thinks that an animal laid his Weetabix as he understands the difference between plants and animals. His growing language skills help him to understand the relationship between the tiny sunflower seed that he sows, and the giant sunflower that grows three months later.

Children need to hear language for different reasons in order to use language for different reasons. Young children are learning to use language:

- **To develop relationships:** children use language to form connections with other children and adults. They learn how to become a confident individual in a group, to collaborate and cooperate, to understand social expectations and boundaries.

- **To understand, express and manage feelings:** children learn to name different emotions, which helps them to understand and regulate their feelings and behaviour.

- **To think and learn:** children use increasingly complex language to obtain and convey information; to organise and express their thinking; to reflect, evaluate and plan in a purposeful way; and to develop their conceptual understanding of the world.

- **To be creative:** children use language to express curiosity and inventiveness and to develop and represent their ideas.

> *I love going to forest school when it's raining. I stick my tongue out and catch the raindrops.*

Language, learning and play

Language skills support all aspects of the Early Years curriculum. The small but real gender gap in toddlers' verbal skills widens in the pre-school years (Eliot 2012: 131), impacting on boys' attainment, which is lower than girls' attainment in all areas of learning and development at the end of the EYFS in England (DfE 2014b). So how can we support boys' language development to prevent them from being disadvantaged in school?

All children have an intentional drive to learn through play and exploration. It is through their play that children explore and act out their interests and preoccupations, and it is in their play that they become confident, experimental and competent language users. In Chapter 5, we saw that boys' play is often active, fluid and takes them away from adults who could be supporting their learning, as we see in the following scenario.

Three boys are painting a fence in the reception class garden with coloured water. There is a tray containing the coloured water on one side of the tarmac area and the fence is on the other side. The boys dip their brushes in the tray of water, race across the tarmac to the fence, 'paint' the fence, then race back to dip their brushes in again. They could have taken the tray of coloured water over to the fence, but it was much more fun to run backwards and forwards across the tarmac.

It is likely that gender differences in play amplify girls' small, initial advantage in language skills. 'Simply put, girls spend more time talking, drawing, and role-playing in relational ways, whereas boys spend more time moving, targeting, building, and role-playing as heroes . . . the reason boys don't read and write as well as girls has little to do with innate brain wiring and everything to do with the reality that girls engage more than boys with words' (Eliot 2011). If this is the case, how can we provide more language opportunities in boys' physically active play?

3 Who shall we talk to? The role of the adult

Babies and young children learn to communicate with their first carers. Research by Tizard and Hughes (1984) showed that children learn language very effectively in the home, with caring adults who are interested in what they have to say and who model language in everyday situations.

Over the first few years of life, children become better able to distinguish and articulate subtle differences in the sound system of their language, *phonology*, as the muscles in their face and mouth develop. The more practice they have at talking, the better their muscles develop, so young children need adults around them who encourage them to talk and who listen and respond with interest.

Grammar, *syntax*, becomes more accurate and children absorb the underlying rules of their language when they hear adults modelling language and when they are confident to experiment with language themselves.

Children acquire *semantic* skills when adults listen and respond to their attempts to express themselves, and help them to interpret the spoken and written language of other people.

They learn the *pragmatics* of their language by interacting with different groups of people in different contexts.

> Mark is playing in the construction area with some small animals and hollow blocks. He looks up when an adult approaches and delightedly tells her about his play:
> *Them koalas are way scary. The baddies kicked them in the nuggets.*

In this example, Mark has picked up the local dialect (phonology), the local syntax ('them koalas') and he can express meaning, semantics, in colourful language that he has presumably heard at home. He still has something to learn about the appropriateness of certain language in some contexts (pragmatics)!

Practice makes perfect

Language in = Language out.

(Eliot 2012)

This astonishing feat of learning depends on the mediation of adults who model language skills and who inspire children to become joyful communicators. A study in Oxfordshire found that children were most relaxed and keen to talk in places where there was no adult agenda, for example, at snack time, when they were doing up shoelaces, making models or playing with dough (Fisher 2016). In adult-led situations, there can be a tendency for adults to control and direct the talk towards certain goals. Children get better at talking by talking, so the adult role should be to model language skills, to facilitate children to talk to each other, and to encourage children to take a leading role in a conversation with an adult or with their peers. How much of the day can children actively talk and listen, rather than passively?

How can we plan for the different ways that boys and girls acquire language?

In Early Years settings, where practitioners are predominantly female, adults can inadvertently spend more time interacting with girls, as Gussin Paley found: 'When the children separate by sex, I, the teacher, am often on the girls' side. We move at the same pace and reach for the same activities, while the boys barricade them-selves in the blocks, periodically making forays into female territory' (Gussin Paley 1984: ix).

Adults can prevent the gender gap in language skills from widening in the Early Years by:

- tuning into boys' preoccupations and play preferences, developing an awareness 'of the child . . . in the moment' (Rose and Rogers 2012: 54);
- proactively engaging with boys' play and supporting their social language and language for learning in non-threatening, everyday contexts;
- giving children autonomy in their learning: all children learn best when they are intrinsically motivated, and boys are often more reluctant than girls to do an activity for a teacher (Cigman 2014);
- helping children to develop language that will allow them to understand, express and manage their feelings: boys' later language development impacts on their development of impulse control or self-regulation. Rose and Rogers (2012: 54–5)

refer to a process they call 'co-regulation', when the adult 'communicates their understanding and empathy as well as addressing the child's need', laying 'the foundation for *self-regulation*';

- modelling specific language that children can use to create positive interactions with other children and adults, as well as language for learning;

Hamsa is standing next to the sandpit watching Rashid and Reuben, who are digging a deep hole. He clearly wants to join in, but isn't sure how to go about it.

He picks up a handful of sand and throws it at Rashid, who responds with an annoyed grunt. Hamsa throws another handful of sand at the two boys. Rashid kicks some sand at Hamsa and Reuben shouts: *Hey, stop chucking sand.* Their teacher comes over and says to Hamsa: *Do you want to play with Rashid and Reuben? You could go and say, 'can I help you dig the hole?'* Hamsa repeats the teacher's words, Reuben gives him a spade and they all carry on digging. A few minutes later, Hamsa calls over to the teacher: *Come and see our hole, we're the best diggers!* Rashid echoes: *Yeh, we're the best diggers!*

- introducing new vocabulary through books, songs, visits, explorations and discoveries: children absorb new vocabulary easily when it connects with their experience. Adults can scaffold children's learning, for example modelling specific language relating to mathematical and scientific concepts, such as *float, sink, heavy* and *light* in playful situations. Children learn how one word can be used differently in different contexts: *light* as a feather, *light* blue, switch on the *light*, supporting them to move from receptive language (comprehension) to expressive language;
- 'planting' an idea, a resource, a new word or a question to encourage language and interactions.

Adults and children learning together

Sustained shared thinking has been associated with high-quality early learning environments (Sylva et al. 2004). It involves shared conversations and experiences between children or between adults and children that lead to active co-construction of knowledge to solve a problem, make new discoveries or explore and uncover new understandings. Children can practise:

- using language to explain;
- giving instructions;

- arguing a point of view or persuading;
- using language to describe and retell events and stories.

The specific role of the adult is to:

- listen and observe, tuning into children's language and actions;
- show genuine interest;
- respect and support children's decisions and choices, and offer alternative suggestions;
- recap and clarify children's thoughts and ideas, and offer alternative viewpoints;
- recast and expand child's words, extending children's vocabulary and modelling more advanced sentence structure;
- model curiosity and ways of thinking and help children to develop complex thinking and problem-solving skills;
- ask open-ended questions that encourage children to speculate and hypothesise.

(adapted from Dowling 2005)

Sustained shared thinking can take place at any time, and in many different contexts.

4 Time to talk: some starting points for talking with boys

Children need time in unstructured situations to form relationships, to follow through ideas and to learn to communicate and relate socially. They also benefit from planned opportunities and adults can provide provocations for talking when children can talk about things that are close to home and important to them.

Me, me, me!

- Make a personalised book with photos of a child and scribe the child's comments about their family, their favourite toys and significant experiences.
- Create an alphabet frieze, with pictures and photos of people and things of personal significance to a child.
- Ask children to bring in something from home to talk about. Make a photo display and scribe the things that children say.
- Take photos of significant achievements and display them, to boost boys' sense of pride and status, scribing the child's words: 'I cleaned out the guinea pig hutch today'; 'I can swing across the monkey bars'.

- Create a story with the child as the central character.
- Add details from the child's life to made-up stories: 'So Jack thought, "I'd better eat my porridge before I climb the beanstalk." . . . Oh, did you have porridge for breakfast too? And Jack took some cheese sandwiches with him. You like cheese sandwiches, don't you?'

Everyday experiences and routines

- Snack time: chop fruit, making toast or sandwiches.
- Cooking: make popcorn, bread rolls, pizzas.
- Go to the supermarket to buy ingredients for cooking.
- Polish shoes: provide shoe brushes and cloths and different colour polish.
- Wash up paint pots or cups and plates from snack time.
- Write a postcard, buy a stamp and go to the post box; post it to the child's home . . . and wait for it to arrive!
- Plan activities and trips with the children.
- Tidy up time: introduce a tidy up song.
- Be really clear when giving instructions and use positive statements, not questions: for example, 'I'd like you to . . .'; 'we're all going to . . .'; 'it's time to . . .'.

Mandy took a group of children outside to wash her car with buckets of soapy water and large sponges. The children chatted as they worked:

My dad's got a green taxi.

It's bubbly! (the water) *I popped it! I popped it!*

Me do the wheels.

Playing with language

Children take a particular delight in playing around with the sounds and the meaning of words, creating what Chukovsky calls 'topsy-turvies' (in Whitehead 1997: 74). Children's first jokes can be fun, funny and clever, and toilet humour seems to have a special appeal for boys. Humour also establishes shared meaning, creating a bond between the child and adult when they share their made-up language.

Granny:	Where would you like to go today?
Jacob (age 2):	Poo poo!
Later	
Granny:	Let's get your coat. We're going to poo poo now.
Later	
Mum:	Did you have a fun time at poo poo?

Children need to be able to make *sense* before the can create *nonsense* (Meek, in Moyles 1999: 48): they show their knowledge of something by subverting it with nonsense words.

Jay, age 4, drops his card under the table. He crouches down to find it, but can't see it: *It must have been taken by a card napper.*

5 Where shall we talk? Creating language-rich spaces and places

We are building up a picture of boys who love to be active and who can be very sociable but might need some additional support with their language and self-regulation skills. How can places and spaces be developed to support boys' language and communication? The only way to find out is to observe and track the boys! This allows us to create an environment that encourages talking and thinking in the places where boys choose to go. Different children feel comfortable and at ease in different types of environments.

Interactive spaces and spaces to be alone or with a friend

Boys and girls need time to be quiet and reflective as well as being active and noisy. We can encourage children to interact and communicate by creating areas for collaborative work, large enough for a group of children to work together.

At other times, adults can interact with quieter children, giving them a chance to talk about their work, interests and feelings.

Some places and spaces that encourage language and interaction can include:

- a large sand pit, where children can plan and create together;
- a movement/soft play area to encourage rough and tumble play for boys and girls;
- places where several children can draw and make together: large chalkboards and whiteboards; an interactive whiteboard on the wall; large sheets of paper on tables and on the floor; mats on the floor;

- a workshop area and construction area for large-scale model-making with recycled materials and hollow blocks; display photos of the children's models to encourage children to plan and reflect with each other and with adults;
- put books in different areas that connect with children's play, for example books about building and vehicles in the construction and small world areas;
- create 'talking spaces' where children go to debate and discuss, such as a 'piazza' or an arena;
- provide heavy loose parts that need more than one child to move them;
- create openings in dens so that children can invite their friends in;
- provide board games that involve turn-taking;
- plan physical games, such as basketball and skittles, where children can set their 'PB', their 'personal best', as well as compete with other children.

Role-play areas

Play . . . is story in action, just as storytelling is play put into narrative form.

(Gussin Paley 1991: 4)

Socio-dramatic play has a central role in enabling children to move from concrete to abstract thinking. It's exciting and compelling and lets children discover and experiment with different ways of being that are both themselves and not themselves.

Children's dramatic play starts with make-believe actions: pretending to make a cup of tea or feed a doll. It develops into symbolic play with make-believe objects: squirting water on a fire with a stick.

Children's storytelling develops as they create a make-believe situation that can be verbalised.

> Henry: *Just have to get something for the dragon's den.*

Dramatic play becomes socio-dramatic play when other children join in, to create action, a more complex plot and different characters. Drama and role play develop out of familiar stories, and they give children the experience of switching roles and ways of being.

> Wilfred is playing on a 'pirate ship': *I'm Captain Roger and Dariusz is my helper. I have to steer and sometimes I go in the cabin.*

> Ethan: *If someone's been naughty, we write them down and put them in jail.*
> Joseph: *. . . and Spiderman tells them off.*

When children have permanent access to high-quality open-ended resources, this supports symbolic play, as they can respond flexibly by using the same materials in different ways, as well as revisiting resources and ideas.

> Mitchell is making a model with recycled boxes: *That's where the fire comes out, that's where the person sits and that's where the controls are.*

In the scenario below, the boys are working things out and developing the rules of the game as they go along. Their play is flexible and fluid and they revise and adapt their ideas.

> Blake: *Pretend I got lost with you, didn't I?*
> Michael: *No, you got lost on your own. Then you said, 'Mama, mama, save me . . .'*
>
> *(continued)*

(continued)

He lifts up a dinosaur: *Rooooaaaaaarrrrr.*

Blake: *I'm going to get a different dinosaur.*

Michael: *Yes, but it has to be a little one.*

He follows Blake to the box of dinosaurs and helps him find a small one.

Michael: *This time you have a longer tail. Then mine goes away, then yours.*

Both boys push the dinosaurs around and around the mat, making roaring noises, then they make them play fight.

Blake: *I actually want to be a different dinosaur.*

Michael: *Okay, do you want to be a hider in the woods? He just runs really fast!* He gives Blake another dinosaur.

We can support boys' language development by dipping in and out of their socio-dramatic play, making a suggestion or a comment, providing a resource and by showing interest in their characters and storyline, without taking over the play. Children might like to use a video or voice recorder to record their play, appealing to boys who are technologically minded, and they can add a voiceover or text to the recording.

The Social Play Continuum

Franklin and Jackson are playing in the sand tray when an adult walks past.

Franklin: *Do you know what we're making? We're making a house.*

Jackson: *We're making an office. You start with a volcano and you smooth it off at the top and at the side. That's our office.*

Adult: *You work in a volcano?!*

Jackson: *Yeh, it's an office volcano.*

The Social Play Continuum was devised as a result of research into links between children's play and learning and is an observational tool that can be used by researchers and practitioners to evaluate the quality of children's play and learning. The research identified four domains in children's play: the associative domain, the social domain, the highly social domain and the cooperative domain, 'each characterised by increasingly complex language and action' (Broadhead, in Broadhead et al. 2010: 43). There is a clear link between language and learning in the cooperative domain, which involves reciprocal language and action, and is the type of play where intellectual challenge is the greatest.

> When play is thematically driven by the children, the opportunities to follow their own interests and preoccupations means that play is more likely to be located within the Co-operative Domain with its characteristic, rich use of language, problem-solving and reciprocity.
>
> (Broadhead, in Broadhead et al. 2010: 54)

Children move through the domains as their language and experiences grow, and when they enjoy an environment that provides freely accessible, open-ended resources, alongside adults who model and plant ideas, ways of thinking and specific resources that help to develop children's play. Broadhead's research showed that there was more play in the cooperative domain in nursery than in reception, where nursery children had more space and time for child-initiated play.

'Whatever you want it to be' place

Vinny is playing in a dark tent in his pre-school, with two rubber duck torches. He quacks and dives into the tent.

Do you know what I'm doing with these (ducks)? *I'm throwing them! They're fighting.*

He takes the batteries out of one torch, puts them back in and screws the end back on, very competently. The torch doesn't work.

The batteries are the wrong way round. He takes them out again, turns them round and puts the end back on. The torch works.

Evelyn joins him:	*I'm the mummy and you're the brother. Brother! It's bedtime!*
Vinny:	*Already?*
Evelyn:	*It's nearly bedtime, brother. No, it's morning time.*
Vinny (impatiently):	*Is it bedtime or morning time? I'm just trying to fix this, okay? I've fixed it, that's gonna be glued on, it goes along okay now, it does.*

Open-ended resources allow play to change and adapt over time and are the 'most transformative' (Broadhead, in Broadhead et al. 2010: 46) as children can use them in a variety of ways, which can connect with and extend their experiences and interests. They allow all children to bring their wider social and cultural experiences into the setting. The highest levels of play in the cooperative domain were found in the open-ended role-play area, fittingly called the 'whatever you want it to be place' by a child. Resources for an open-ended role-play area, or the 'whatever you want it to be place', can include:

- fabrics of different colours and textures;
- cardboard boxes – different sizes, some big enough to climb in;
- netting;
- cardboard tubes;
- corrugated cardboard;
- cable bobbins;
- cotton wool;
- clothes pegs, building clips;
- silver foil;
- sticky tape;
- marker pens;
- shells / feathers, etc.;
- ice cream tubs.

What have children created in the 'whatever you want it to be place'?

- The Channel Tunnel: Shaun ran under a large piece of material through the opening at one end and ran out the other side speaking 'French': 'Hey you guys!'.
- The Big Bad Wolf's house.
- A barbecue.
- A bear hunt.
- A tsunami.
- A magic shed.
- A spaceship.
- A train-house.

- A lookout.
- A dragon's den.
- And more. . . . !

6 Parents

> For all children, the quality of the home learning environment is more important for intellectual and social development than parental occupation, education or income. What parents do is more important than who parents are.
>
> (Sylva et al. 2004: ii)

Strong links with parents, supported by a keyperson, enable schools and Early Years settings to give children the most positive start to their educational experience. Parents can help practitioners to support their child's language development by sharing information about the strengths, experiences and interests of their child, information that the boys, especially, might struggle to communicate without their special family member to interpret. Schools and settings can share ideas of ways in which parents can support their child to influence the language experiences that children have at home. Promote conversations with families by making:

- learning stories: share children's experiences in the setting and at home in a special book that children can look at alone or with a friend or parent;
- an *'ask us about . . .'* board with photos of things that the children have been doing at home and in the setting;
- *'just to let you know that at home I . . .'* sheets: ask parents to share stories about special things that they've done at home.

Conclusion

> Verbalizing our thoughts and organizing rational speech and writing are the demanding preoccupations of a lifetime.
>
> (Whitehead 1997: 61)

Becoming an active communicator is a long process that requires sensitive support. In this chapter we have seen that it is possible to override gender differences in the development of early language skills through interaction with encouraging, responsive and inspiring adults in a stimulating and enabling environment. In the final two chapters, we explore ways of promoting boys' learning across all areas of the curriculum.

Summary

- Early language development is influenced more strongly by the environment than by a child's sex.

- Stimulate early language development by giving status to boys' interests in conversations.

- Create opportunities to talk that are purposeful, link to children's experiences and that reflect their home cultures.

- Provide an environment with access to interactive and open-ended resources that children can use playfully and creatively, with sensitive support by an adult.

7 Planning for cross-curricular learning

Introduction

Blake (age 4½) is wearing his North Pole explorer's outfit: a woolly hat, a warm, padded waistcoat and his explorer's backpack. He is tracking polar bears in his garden, and is very excited, as he's just spotted an arctic fox through his cardboard tube binoculars. It's hot outside, and he comes inside for a drink of water.

He changes into a straw hat and cotton waistcoat, puts his explorer's backpack on again and calls his mother to come into his 'time machine': *I'm going back in time to a really, really long, long time ago, to a billion years, I need to find the dinosaur that's not really a dinosaur. He lives in the desert. He's not dangerous, he's a plant eater.*

Blake has been playing 'explorers' for well over a year, at home and at his nursery, and his play has evolved over this time as his language and his knowledge and understanding have grown, with the help of adults who have encouraged and supported his interest. He wholeheartedly enters into the world that he creates every time he plays North Pole explorers or desert explorers, and as he revisits the play, he constructs his learning at a greater depth. His fascination with explorers has led him to absorb knowledge about climate differences and appropriate clothing for different climates; animals, their habitats and the food that they eat; as well as an understanding of recent time and 'a long, long time ago'.

In previous chapters, we focused on creating a learning environment that supports children's language, fine motor control and self-regulation: areas of development where there can be some disadvantage for boys. These developmental areas are fundamental to all aspects of learning, for all children and, in England, they come under the Prime Areas of Learning in the EYFS: communication and language development, physical development and personal, social and emotional development (DfE 2014a).

In this chapter we consider how we can plan a learning environment that builds on the Prime Areas, where children can develop scientific and mathematical knowledge, skills and understanding and where they can become geographers and historians, creative artists and critical thinkers, and join the 'literacy club' (Smith 1988) as confident readers and writers. In the EYFS, these come under the specific areas of learning: understanding the world, mathematical development, literacy and expressive arts and design (DfE 2014a).

1 'Whatever you want to become' learning

Arthur, age 23 months, is sitting having tea with his mother. He screws up his eyes against the bright light outside, points out of the window and says: *Light.*

His mother nods, and says: *Yes, it's a sunny day. I wonder where the sun goes when it's dark at night.*

Arthur thinks for a moment and says: *Bed.*

Babies are born with the innate drive and capacity to question, hypothesise and learn from experience. Arthur is building his understanding of the world through an interactive process called social constructivism (Vygotsky 1978). He draws on his limited experience, and as his experience grows, he will accommodate new ideas and information and assimilate them into an expanding view of the world (Piaget 1957). This can happen very naturally at home, where children learn about the real world and they learn about possible worlds through conversations with parents and carers in everyday activities, at bath time, at mealtimes, when they are out and about in the buggy or playing inside or in the garden (Tizard and Hughes 1984).

As children move into Early Years settings, they encounter practitioners who make deliberate and intentional decisions about the learning environment and the learning opportunities that they provide. The environment that practitioners create will reflect their pedagogy and their image of the child.

The image of the child

We say all children are rich . . . All children whatever their culture, whatever their lives are rich, better equipped, more talented, stronger and more intelligent than we can suppose.

(Malaguzzi, quoted in Moss 2016)

Loris Malaguzzi was founder of the Reggio Emilia educational philosophy. He believed that children have 'one hundred languages' that reflect the many ways that children see, explore and respond to the world, each child in their unique way.

The child
is made of one hundred.
The child has
a hundred languages
a hundred hands
a hundred thoughts
a hundred ways of thinking
of playing, of speaking.

A hundred always a hundred
ways of listening
of marveling, of loving
a hundred joys
for singing and understanding
a hundred worlds
to discover
a hundred worlds
to invent
a hundred worlds
to dream.

(Loris Malaguzzi, translated by Leila Gandini, in Edwards et al. 2011)

There is a danger that we can stifle children's unique responses to the world by planning for narrow and prescriptive outcomes, placing a lid on children's capabilities. This kind of teaching is 'a complete humiliation for children's ingenuity and potential' (Moss 2016). This view is supported by a survey commissioned by Ofsted to identify qualities of good practice in supporting early learning. The survey found that, in the best settings, practitioners:

> did not think of teaching and play as separate endeavours. In every playful encounter we observed, adults, consciously or otherwise, were teaching. They were making important decisions about the resources they used and the questions they asked. They thought carefully about their physical behaviours, the language they used and the environments they created.

(Ofsted 2015: 5)

Supporting development and learning

We can nurture children's 'hundred languages' and playful learning by:

- providing an environment with natural materials and genuinely purposeful activities that allows children to investigate the real world in depth;
- creating challenging learning opportunities that have intrinsic motivation, enabling children to build their own learning pathways;

- co-constructing learning alongside children, where adults inspire, listen, model enjoyment of the thinking and learning process, and offer specific learning strategies and skills (Dowling 2005);

- using observations of children and the environment to decide when, where and how to support children's play;

- promoting flexible, 'possibility thinking' (Craft, in Stewart 2011), facilitating understanding, not asking for or giving the 'right' answer;

- asking: 'whose thinking is represented here?' 'How much scope is there for children to find their own ways to represent and develop their own ideas?' (Stewart 2011: 83);

- providing constructive feedback;

- encouraging reflection, giving children time to speculate and wonder, test things out and revise and adapt their ideas.

All children have an entitlement to 'possibility thinking'. They should be allowed to express their ideas individually as well as taking account of different perspectives. A learning environment that promotes possibility thinking is effective for all children, and it allows practitioners to respond to the active and energetic style of learning that many boys demand: creating powerful learners who are willing to take risks in their learning, revise their ideas and try new things, who can respond to challenges, struggle and overcome difficulties, and gain a sense of achievement and satisfaction.

2 Planning the learning environment

A suitable learning environment for investigators, problem-solvers and creative thinkers will give children time and continuously accessible, flexible resources to initiate their own play, in which they can explore, experiment, revisit, and become intentional in their actions. There should also be some new and unexpected 'provocations' for learning. These might be new materials or familiar materials juxtaposed in unfamiliar places to prompt and inspire discussion and debate and help to challenge and extend children's possibility thinking. Practitioners will be both responsive to children's moments of excitement and wonder, and proactive in their planning.

Planning in the moment

Some events are broadly predictable, although we might not know exactly when they are going to happen. For example, we know that there will be windy and snowy days and we can provide active learning opportunities that link to these predictable events, such as making kites on a windy day or creating a 'winter Olympics' outside in the snow. There will also be unpredictable events that can lead to exciting new learning. The alert practitioner will respond to the unpredictable comment or event with planning in the moment, with a group of children or with one child. It might involve a brief interaction, for example with a child who has discovered a snail: 'We could find a box for your snail. What shall we put in the box to make the snail feel comfortable and at home?' It might involve a combination of immediate planning and planning over time:

Lukas notices a butterfly flapping against a window. His teacher stops the group phonics session and responds to the children's excitement and curiosity. He recognises the potential learning and wonder in this experience:

- The teacher catches the butterfly gently and holds it in his cupped hands while the children look closely. They talk about its delicate wings, and how they need to handle it carefully. They look at the colours and patterns on the wings.
- He tells them some fascinating facts: butterflies taste with their feet, and they can't fly when they're cold.
- After the group session, he puts some colourful material outside and the children make 'wings' and run around 'tasting' the daisies in the grass, the leaves and the puddles with their feet!
- They take cameras, clipboards and binoculars outside and they take photos and draw the butterflies that they see.
- Over the next few days, they look up some more interesting facts about butterflies in books and on the interactive whiteboard.
- They decide to grow some flowers that attract butterflies.
- Some children learn how to make symmetry paintings, and they talk about symmetrical patterns while they finger paint.
- They discover that they can buy some caterpillars that will arrive in a jar so that they can watch them turn into butterflies. One child writes a letter to place an order.
- And of course they all read *The Hungry Caterpillar* by Eric Carle!

In-the-moment planning helps to strengthen relationships between adults and children and it boosts children's self-confidence, when practitioners show an interest in their discoveries and fascinations. It's a good time for a conversation, supporting children's language development as well as their burgeoning understanding of the world.

As well as in-the-moment planning, we can 'plan for spontaneity' by predicting children's interests, based on our observations and conversations with children and their families, and preparing resources that children can access independently to support these interests when they emerge in their play.

Planning for boys' predictable interests

We can harness a range of boys' predictable interests to develop learning in all curriculum areas.

Dens

In Chapter 2, we noted that boys are more likely than girls to take their play away from adults. This can take them into bushes, behind sheds and behind sofas. There can be plenty of good learning in play away from adults, but potential learning can be missed, leading to low-level and unconstructive play when it is unobserved and unsupervised.

The potential for learning when children create dens and when adults support the play is boundless, for example:

- **Maths, science and expressive arts and design:** boys can extend their imaginative play, making a bear lair, a fairy grotto or a dragon's den with non-prescriptive materials of different shapes, sizes and weights; they can use wood, plastic, material and metal, learning about the properties of different materials; they can build up their stamina as learners by planning and designing dens and sharing plans and designs with others.
- **Language skills:** using complex language to discuss plans and ideas; working collaboratively, using language to explain, persuade and negotiate, to describe and narrate.
- **Learning dispositions:** sustaining play over time with deep levels of involvement.
- **Literacy skills:** reading and writing books linked to the den-building and writing for many different purposes, such as making signs, labels and posters.

Pirates

This is a powerful predictable interest for boys that has the potential for learning across the curriculum:

- **Maths, science, literacy and expressive arts and design:** make a pirate shop and label and price pirate clothes, peg legs, glass eyes, hooks, patches, parrot food, weevil catchers, grog.
- **Language skills:** learn pirate language (www.speakpirate.com) and pirate songs.
- **Literacy skills:** write the ship's log, messages in bottles, job descriptions for the Cap'n and other pirates, menus, lists of supplies for the voyage; read and write stories about pirates.
- **Self-regulation skills:** apply for a weapons licence, make wanted posters and write accident reports.
- **Science, maths and geography:** make weather charts and treasure maps.
- **Mathematical language:** go on treasure hunts.

Austen: *I've found some treasure, it's <u>that</u> big.* (He holds his fingers very close together.) *It's invisible.*

Journeys and explorers

Context: ten 4-year-old children take part in the following piece of work over a few weeks, during group times with their teacher in a reception class.

The teacher introduces the idea of making a journey to a new and undiscovered land.

They talk about different ways that they could make the long journey: by boat, train or car (but only as far as the sea . . .), by airplane, by air balloon, by submarine, by rocket . . . They decide to go by boat and they draw the boat and give it a name: *Brave Explorer.*

They all think of something useful to take with them: seeds to grow food, tools for digging and weeding, a cow for milk, a sheep for wool, a sewing kit, warm and waterproof hats, sun cream.

They all choose something precious to take with them: a teddy, a favourite book, a favourite toy, a pet rabbit, a baby sister.

They talk about what they might find when they arrive in the undiscovered land: sand and desert by the sea, jungle and mountains inland.

They decide what they will do first: build a house, fence in the animals, fetch firewood, collect water and sow seeds.

They write some postcards home, describing the journey and the new land.

Children can go on to develop this 'explorer' play in many different ways in their self-initiated play, expressing their 'hundred languages':

- **Maths, science, literacy and expressive arts and design:** making small model vehicles inside and large 'role play' vehicles outside; cooking in mud kitchens and sowing some vegetable seeds; going on 'wild animal hunts'.
- **Literacy skills:** making individual and group books, using photos taken in their play, and their own drawings and writing; making passports.
- **Geography:** making maps and looking at a globe.

Making and mending

> When the children come into their reception class at the beginning of the day, Henry and Marlow notice a box on a table containing different types of keys and locks. They whoop with delight and tip the contents onto the table.
>
> They sit together in silence, trying each key in turn in the different locks. Marlow finds a key that turns one of the locks, and he whoops again.
>
> *Look, Henry, look, look, it's working!*
>
> Henry carries on trying the keys until he finds one that matches a lock, and then he imitates Marlow's whoop. *Look, look! Yeh, I done it!*

Many boys are fascinated by the way things work, and enjoy building things and taking them apart. We can encourage boys and girls to explore how things are made and enjoy building and creating by providing:

- small, broken electrical and electronic items that children can take apart and put back together: computer keyboards, circuit boards, mobile phones, toasters, radios, plugs, sockets, with screwdrivers and instruction sheets;
- small bulbs and bulb holders, wire and screwdrivers to make a simple electrical circuit;
- clipboards, paper and pencils so that children can record their findings;
- provide goggles and talk about health and safety issues: electricians and repair mechanics have to follow safety rules and work in a safe environment;
- make health and safety posters.

A 'making and mending' station will give children opportunities to develop:

- **Scientific and mathematical skills and understanding:** talking about similarities and differences, understanding how to create a simple electrical circuit, hypothesising and checking out their ideas: *how do light bulbs work? Can I make a light bulb light up?*
- **Literacy skills:** recording ideas, looking up information in books.
- **Expressive arts and design:** making a robot with flashing eyes or a lighthouse.

Traditional tales

Traditional tales involve plenty of conflict, competition and challenging behaviour that can appeal to boys!

- **Little Red Riding Hood:** make 'wanted' posters for the Big, Bad Wolf; make a map of the route to granny's house through the forest.
- **Three Little Pigs:** set up a building site with straw, sticks and bricks, a cement mixer and tools to build a house; make architects' plans for the houses.
- **Three Billy Goats Gruff:** write a newspaper report about the incident when the biggest Billy Goat Gruff overcame the Troll (the adult will scribe for the children); build a bridge across some guttering or across the water tray. *How can I make it long enough? How can I make it strong enough to carry the goats?*
- **Create a 'crime scene' based on a story:** children can make detective badges and role-play the different characters.

Seasons and the weather

Outdoor spaces can be used dynamically and flexibly. They change with the seasons, and can be unpredictable. Instead of simply talking about a daily weather chart, children will learn so much more about the changing environment over the year by being outside!

- Children can experience the changes in the weather, feeling the effect of the wind on their faces, their clothes and their hair; describing warm winds and cold winds; discovering how they can walk up a snowy slope, slide down an icy slope and keep their balance on a muddy slope. They can discover that the rain butt is full after a downpour.

> Christy is new to his nursery. His teacher, Tim, shows him how to collect some water from the water butt in his bucket, making sure that the drip tray is underneath the tap. Tim explains that Christy can help himself to water, and they have a chat about using water carefully, as it is a valuable natural resource.

- Children can observe and ask questions about changes caused by the weather, and use language to question and clarify their ideas. They can develop systems for investigating and recording findings in an organised way. They can watch the trees bend over in the wind, and see eaves and small branches blown to the ground. They can ask: *Is the surface slippery today? How deep is the muddy puddle under the tree? What happens to a rain puddle on a freezing cold day? What happens to ice when we bring it indoors? Where do puddles go on a hot day? Where do shadows come from? Can I make a shadow?*

- They can play in mud kitchens, dig in wet and dry soil and sand, make a family of snow people, play in the water or find shade on a hot day, find shelter from the wind on a blustery day, sit under a sheet of clear plastic and watch and listen to the rain falling. *Add powder paint to the plastic sheet for a special effect!*

- They can make kites and windmills that move in the wind, help build a fire on a still, cold day and create a shady shelter for themselves or for stuffed toys on a sunny day.

- They can help to grow vegetables and water them on a hot day; they can make soups and salads with ingredients from the vegetable garden, and eat them, gaining a genuine sense of purpose as well as developing a sense of responsibility for living things; they can handle and smell real vegetables in a role-play shop or market stall.

Cooking

> Eddie (age 5): *We're having a barbecue. Not a real one.*
>
> Lennon: *A real one.* He rubs two pieces of bark together. *Is this how you make fire?*

Be adventurous with cooking activities to engage active boys:

- Make popcorn in a saucepan inside or in two metal sieves over an open fire. What else can you cook over an open fire? Talk about the fire drill, safety rules and make safety posters. Have a fire extinguisher and sand buckets to hand.

- Make bread or pizza dough and watch it rise.

- Make food for a giant (a giant sandwich) and food for tiny creatures.
- Mix drinking chocolate into play dough and trick people by making a box of play dough chocolates!
- Cook home-grown vegetables from the vegetable garden.
- Create a mud kitchen with funnels, jugs, pots and pans, kitchen utensils, bowls; provide labelled jars of natural materials to add to the mud and boxes so that children can collect leaves, stones, twigs and other natural materials themselves.

Making pizza: what are children learning?

Literacy: reading and writing recipes; making a shopping list of ingredients; finding the ingredients by reading the packets; writing an invitation to a pizza party; writing orders for pizza delivery.

Maths: counting and quantity: *I've got five slices of salami*; talking about the size and shape of the pizza; using positional language: *next to, under*.

Science: predicting and discovering how the dough changes by adding yeast and cooking it.

IT: making and printing a recipe book and photos with instructions on how to make a pizza.

. . . as well as language and personal, social and emotional development, making choices, stating preferences, working with other children and adults;

. . . and physical development, making and kneading the dough, and riding the bikes to deliver the pizzas.

Planning for routines

Everyday routines at home have the potential to help children learn so much about numbers, size and quantity, everyday purposes for writing and reading, knowledge about how the weather changes and how the environment changes in different types of weather and so much more. In the same way, we can use everyday routines in our settings to support mathematical development, science and literacy:

- **At meal and snack times:** *How many potatoes do you want? Do you want half a banana?* Talk about healthy food and make menus.
- **At self-registration:** children can peg their names on a line, to develop fine motor strength and independence, as well as recognising their name: *You're the first to find your name . . . Your name and Sam's name both start with an S.*

- **Putting on boots:** *Oops, one wellie is bigger than the other. Let's find two the same size . . . You'll be able to splash in the puddles now!*

- **Tidying up:** match different shape and size blocks to pictures on a shelf: *Will the Lego fit into the crate?*

As well as using children's predictable interests to support their learning, observational assessment of individual children helps practitioners to plan from, and respond to, their fluid interests. It also allows us to identify styles of play and respond to support learning.

3 Responding to children's schematic play

Children commonly display specific and repeated styles of play or 'schema'. Athey defines schema as 'patterns of behaviour and thinking in children' (2007: 5) and we can observe children's schema in their language, play themes, behaviour, drawings and movement. Children repeat actions that fit into specific schema while they investigate and experiment:

- **Transporting:** the child who likes to empty a cupboard and take the contents to the other end of the room.

- **Trajectory:** the child who pushes cars and trains along the floor, and the child who enjoys throwing and kicking a ball.

- **Enclosing or enveloping:** the child who likes to sit under the table, or wrap himself in a cape or cloak; the child who likes to fill bags and boxes or put animals inside enclosures.

- **Rotational:** the child who loves circular movement, running round and round trees, spinning and twirling; the child who is fascinated by wheels and windmills.
- **Connecting:** the child who lines bricks up across a room and who enjoys making train tracks.

Some schematic play can be problematic, for example when a child hurls or kicks objects (trajectory) or persistently empties cupboards and leaves toys in the bushes at the far end of the garden (transporting). The active type of play that boys seem to love can take up a lot of space. It might be trajectory or rotational: play-fighting and rough and tumble; football and other ball games; racing around a track on a bike. It can be transporting or connecting: moving bricks in a wheelbarrow across the outside area, or laying a train track across the floor where other children might be trying to play. Boys who have an enclosing schema might choose to hide in bushes and dens away from an adult.

Children need to learn to move, throw and kick in a controlled way and they need to learn to move and store objects appropriately. Many children move in and out of different schema, but if a persistent schema is identified, suitable space, resources and activities can be provided to support the child to develop their thinking and understanding through their schematic play. Repeated schematic behaviour helps to create connections in the brain that embed learning.

We can harness children's schematic play as they explore and learn about the physical and biological world, giving children space and time to discover how different materials behave and to develop scientific thinking, testing out their ideas and making significant breakthroughs. They can express their creativity by making new connections and finding inventive solutions.

The following activities support children with different schema to investigate the natural world, and to experience and gain an understanding of mathematical concepts.

Trajectory

- Make popcorn.
- Scatter seeds, water them and watch them germinate and grow.
- Make a volcano with vinegar and baking soda.
- Make a rocket and launch it!
- Dig for treasure in the sandpit.
- Make trails and patterns with spray bottles and washing-up liquid bottles.
- Put a long sheet of paper under a swing, swing backwards and forwards and drip or splatter paint on the paper.
- Hammer and saw wood at the woodwork bench.
- Knock down skittles.
- How many ways can a drum be played? Use spoons, sticks and feathers as beaters or throw ping pong balls to make different sounds.

Transporting

- Make a pulley in the sandpit.
- Move logs to make a seating area.
- Empty the water or sand tray.
- Pour water down guttering.
- 'Fish' for numbers, shapes and interesting objects: on a small scale in the water or sand tray, and on a large scale from the slide or climbing frame over a builder's tray.

'Writing on the move' rucksacks are popular for transporting writing materials

Enclosing and enveloping

- Make potions in small containers.
- Sort different-sized beakers that fit together like Russian dolls.
- Plant bulbs.
- Bury treasure.
- Make toasted sandwiches.
- Wrap parcels.
- Explore different shape and size materials in a feely box.

Rotational

- Mix play dough, bread dough and make milkshakes.
- Finger painting: try finger painting with drinking chocolate or add different scents to the paint, such as peppermint essence or spices.
- Put water wheels in the water and sand.
- Put the washing in the washing machine and watch it go round and round.
- Turn the tap on and off.
- Look at a globe.

Connecting

- Build a den.
- Create an obstacle course.
- Make trails with water or stones.
- Build a marble run.
- Make an electrical circuit.

4 Involving parents

The active, adventurous and often unpredictable learning environment outlined in this chapter can pose challenges for some parents. Parents might need to be persuaded of the educational value of such an environment if they have had a very formal education themselves. They might find the idea of 'risky' play, however well it is managed, to be threatening to their child. We can meet parents' concerns by being explicit about the pedagogy behind the planned environment.

- Get all staff on board and make sure that everyone can explain the value of active learning to parents.
- Share your policies and procedures with parents at home visits or visits to the setting before children join you.

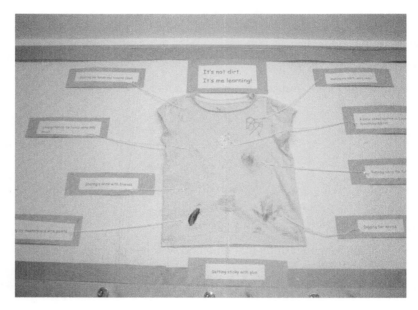

Display for parents explaining the value of messy play

- Display class rules regarding behaviour and safety.
- Display photos of the children playing inside and outside, and annotate the photos using speech bubbles with children's words as they play.
- Use photos and commentary to explain the process of learning, describing how children explore, experiment and adapt their ideas if their plan doesn't work out at first.
- Make learning story books for each child, documenting the process of their learning and their development as a learner as well as their progress in areas of the curriculum.
- Have spare clothes and boots for children.
- Invite parents to come to an open day, a twilight walk or a workshop so that they can experience the learning opportunities that their children are having.

A group of us dads started den-building with the children, but we didn't really need the kids, we were having too much fun ourselves.

Conclusion

> Knowing is a process not a product.
>
> (Bruner 1966: 72)

When a baby is born, the possible futures for the newborn child are limitless. Parents might imagine their child scoring the winning goal in the World Cup, receiving a bouquet on stage in the West End after a magnificent performance or writing the next blockbuster novel. In this chapter, we have explored the central role of proactive and responsive planning in opening up possibilities, allowing boys and girls to be creative and active investigators and problem-solvers so that they can become whatever they want to become.

In the final chapter, we consider some spaces and resources that we can provide to help boys and girls delight in investigating their world.

Summary

- We can nurture children's 'hundred languages' by providing natural materials and genuinely purposeful activities.
- We can promote and extend 'possibility thinking' by creating an exciting and challenging environment with provocations for learning based on children's interests.
- Children's schematic play can be channelled into creative and imaginative learning experiences.

Creating spaces and places to get boys up and running

Introduction

> When he was a child, David Mitchell drew maps. Now he creates worlds.
>
> (Wagner 2014)

The author, David Mitchell, looked back on what he called his first 'novelistic activities' as a child, which involved building worlds by making maps. He recalled 'the pleasure of large sheets of A1 cartridge paper, thick, lovely paper, mounted up on a big echoey mounting board with masking tape so it won't wobble. And I'd cover it with maps.' A different child might have become a cartographer, a travel writer or a geologist. Mitchell was able to combine his early experiences with his unique interests, drive and talents to use his 'world-building' to write novels (Wagner 2014).

In this final chapter, we map out a learning landscape that accounts for the diverse needs of boys and girls: an environment that provides workshops, laboratories, design studios, tinkering studios, offices, kitchens and libraries, where every child can explore options and possibilities that will allow them to be 'whatever they want to be'. We can provide male and female role models of cooks, carers and carpenters, musicians and mathematicians, dancers and doctors, so that any boy or girl believes that they can become a ballet dancer who expresses themselves through movement and music or an accountant who is fascinated by numbers, an astronaut with a drive to explore the vastness of space or a farmer who focuses on cultivating the land.

Room to grow

Bruner states that 'any subject can be taught effectively in some intellectually honest form to any child at any stage of development' (Bruner 1966: 33). This view underpins the concept of the 'spiral curriculum', where children repeatedly revisit ideas and experiences, modifying and deepening their understanding over time. The beginning of any learning journey can start in the early years when children have the opportunity to try out different roles.

1 Young engineers, architects and inventors

Early Years environments should provide rich and playful opportunities where children can observe and experience simple laws of physics, chemistry and mathematics by handling different materials and learning about their properties. Boys often choose to play with blocks and other construction materials. While they are playing, boys and girls can:

- Begin to make predictions about how different materials will behave under different conditions. They can make choices about which materials will be suitable for different purposes.

- Learn about the strength of different materials by handling metals, different types of wood, plastic, wet and dry sand, clay and dough to build and create resources to use in their play. They find out about brittle and pliable materials and discover that a tunnel built with willow can have a curved top, while a tunnel built with large wooden, hollow blocks will have to have a flat top . . . or will it?

- Learn about forces by building a dam, experimenting with sticks, stones, sand and other materials to hold back water.

- Observe that a feather or dandelion seed head will behave in a different way from a brick or a conker when it is dropped from a height.

- Discover that friction affects movement when they push a car along a smooth plastic sheet or a rough area of tarmac.

- Learn that different-shaped objects behave differently by rolling a ball or building with a cylinder.

- Experience gravitational pull, compression and tension when they experiment with different materials to build a bridge that is strong enough to take a toy vehicle.

- Discover that two or more substances can be combined to create a new substance and that different actions affect the way a substance behaves, when they make play dough, drip oil into a puddle or whisk soapflakes into water.

- Encounter real engineering problems to solve: How can I make a mast for my boat, by attaching a tube onto a box, without it falling over? Can I make a bridge that lifts up so that my tall boat can go underneath?

- Develop design skills involving form and function: What materials shall I use to make my boat? How can I make it float? Can I make it strong enough to hold some small world people?

All of the following resources support this learning, inside and outside.

Resources in the continuous provision

- A range of natural materials, such as branches, twigs, logs, shells, leaves and stones;
- wet and dry sand in small and large sand trays and as large a sand pit as possible;
- water, ice and bubbles in small and large trays and a paddling pool;
- buckets, sections of guttering and drainpipe, watering cans.

Attach a clear plastic ramp so that it runs at an angle into a water tray and pour water into the ramp. Experiment with the angle of the ramp and add bends. Put cushions on the ground, so that children can sit underneath and watch the water run down.

Connor, age 3, is watching water moving through a series of channels on a water wall made from bamboo guttering: *It's coming down! I can see it! Aaaaah . . .!* (squealing with delight) *It's there!*

- Earth and compost in small and large trays and a digging area outside;
- dry pasta and rice with water;
- a woodwork bench;
- small and large wooden and plastic blocks in a space that is large enough for a group of at least four children to play together;

(continued)

(continued)

- large-scale and small-scale loose parts (see p. 57 for a list of small- and large-scale resources);
- guttering, drainpipes and ramps with cars and balls and other objects that roll to explore movement (so that boys can express the 'wheel gene' (Eliot 2012) playfully suggests the fascination with wheels that we see in the play of so many boys!);
- a pulley, over the sandpit or over a sand or water tray or a builder's tray;
- different types of small construction toys that connect in different ways;
- magnets and objects made of metal and non-metal;
- resources for dens: large pieces of material of different colours, textures and thicknesses, some that shut out the light and some that let light through; camouflage tarpaulin, shade netting, large emergency blankets or small ones taped together; traffic cones, bamboo canes, crates, guttering, tyres;
- duct tape, string, pegs, clips and hooks to attach and connect materials;
- head and hand torches;
- clipboards and paper for drawing plans.

Places and spaces

- *Create a mechanics workshop* with different size spanners and screwdrivers, nuts and bolts, plugs, old radios and computers to take apart, investigate and mend.
- *Create a model-making area* where children can make space rockets, buses, cars, trains, boats, planes, a hot air balloon . . .
- *Set up a role-play building site* with real bricks, sand and builders' tools.
- *Create an inventors' laboratory* with recycled materials and sensory materials, magnifying glasses, different materials for attaching and connecting, such as string, masking tape, duct tape, paperclips, bulldog clips, Velcro, staplers.
- *Create a chemists' laboratory,* with small bottles and different types of liquids: oils, clear and coloured water, food essences such as vanilla and peppermint, vinegar; ice; powders such as spices, baking powder, cornflour, salt; absorbent and non-absorbent paper and material; goggles, pipettes.
- *Make your own gloop, slime, silly putty.*
- *Set up a light centre,* with a light box, overhead projector, mirrors, torches, colour filters.

A challenge: *Can you make a car move without using your hands?*

2 Young botanists, lepidopterists and zoologists

> Matt brings his dog, Ben, into the children's centre every day. Most of the children love stroking Ben and a few wary children are starting to come closer (especially when they're holding Matt's hand!). The children are learning about Ben's needs – when he is hungry, when he's had enough of the noise and wants some peace and quiet by sitting under a bench or in a bush in the garden, and when he wants to play.
>
> Matt has found that having Ben in the children's centre is a good icebreaker for some of the parents, especially a few of the dads, who are happy to start chatting informally about their children when they come over to stroke Ben.

Early Years gardens can provide the perfect space for children to learn about wildlife and develop a respect for the natural environment. Even tarmac playgrounds will have muddy puddles, leaves and twigs and some wildlife to observe, and city parks, woodland, fields, beaches and streams can all enrich children's experiences.

Children can:

- discover similarities and differences between different creatures when they hunt for different minibeasts (invertebrates . . . children will love the word) under leaves, bark and logs;
- observe patterns and colour in plants and living creatures and learn how some creatures use camouflage to protect themselves. (You can make links between the camouflaged creatures and the camouflage tarpaulin in the den-building area that soldiers use to keep themselves safe.);
- observe animal behaviour, watching a colony of ants cooperating and collaborating to carry food to their nest;
- discover the ingenuity of living creatures as they watch a spider spin a web to catch its food;
- learn about the lifecycle of a butterfly when they spot caterpillars on leaves;
- learn how bees and butterflies need flowers for survival, by setting up a nectar café.

Resources in the continuous provision

- Investigator backpacks, lunchboxes or toolboxes, with binoculars, magnifying glasses, bug boxes, small plastic spoons to pick up insects, small clipboards and notepads, pens and identification sheets. Encourage children to take them into different areas of the garden and spot different creatures and plants;

(continued)

(continued)

- bird, insect, flower and tree identification posters;
- a book box with books about insects, birds, wildflowers and trees to help the children identify different creatures and plants.

Places and spaces

- *Create habitats for different creatures:* a wormery, an ant farm and a bug hotel.
- *Make a nectar café* in a sunny spot, with flowers and herbs that attract butterflies and bees.
- *Keep a pet:* stick insects or land snails inside, a guinea pig or rabbit outside.
- *Set up bird feeders and nesting boxes, and a bird bath.*
- *Create a bird hide:* spot birds and record the birds that you see. Set up a webcam and watch the birds from indoors.
- *Make a pond* in an old sink, investigate standing water in puddles, keep tadpoles or build a mini water garden inside.
- *Create a wild area* with flowers and shrubs that attract butterflies.
- *Develop a sensory garden* with colourful flowers and herbs, with strong scents and different textures.
- *Have a digging area* where children can dig in the earth and find worms.

Two children are bug hunting in their reception garden. They find some insect eggs, and show them to an adult.

Adult: *It's a clear egg, I can't see anything inside.*
Child: *Maybe it's a clever thing, like a lizard, that changes colour.*

Nature detective challenge: Take a camera or a clipboard, paper and pen, and find some hidden treasures to photograph or draw. Look under stones and logs, under the leaves of large plants, on the bark of trees, in puddles . . .

3 Young farmers and cooks

Digging and eating both make a good starting point for inspiring boys!
  Children can:

- learn about root and shoot systems in flower and vegetable plants by sowing seeds in soil and in jars and watching them germinate;
- learn about plant growth by sowing different size seeds, planting bulbs and finding seeds in mature plants, and by watching and measuring the growth of plants such as sunflowers and beans;
- learn about seed dispersal when they find seedlings that have self-germinated;
- discover that plants need light and water by putting them in different places. They can watch seedlings grow towards the light on a window ledge or become weak and spindly in a dark cupboard;
- learn about the seasons, weather changes and develop a sense of time by sowing seeds and watching them grow;
- see how worms break up the soil and other vegetation when they dig in the earth and watch vegetable peelings turn into compost;
- count, measure and compare seeds and the size of plants as they grow;
- write for a purpose, making a gardening book with instructions for sowing seeds and writing labels for plants.

Resources in the continuous provision

- · Different size gardening tools, such as spades and forks, rakes and trowels;
- flowerpots and seed trays;

(continued)

(continued)

- twine, cans and labels for plants;
- trugs and buckets;
- wheelbarrows;
- containers for bulbs and small plants;
- watering cans;
- recipe books and laminated sheets;
- display ground rules: *No licking, no picking! Wash hands after digging.*

Places and spaces

- *Make an edible garden in beds or in pots and containers.* Plant vegetables and edible flowers. Make a scarecrow and tie shiny paper, noisy cans or reflective DVDs on string to scare away the birds. Cook and eat vegetables!
- *Make a mud kitchen* outside and a *role-play kitchen* inside.
- *Make a compost bin.*
- *Build a runner bean* tepee large enough for children to fit inside.
- *Create a role-play market stall* with vegetables that children can handle and talk about before sowing the seeds in the garden. Visit a market or use YouTube videos of markets to extend children's experience. Project a video onto a screen and children can play among the videoed market.
- *Create an observation station*, where children can make close observational drawings of plants and minibeasts.
- *Make a hand washing area* with water and soap, or hand gel.

Challenge: Mark out a square of bare earth and see what you can find in it. You might find worms, stones, weeds, leaves . . . anything else?

4 Young musicians, artists and performers

It must not be forgotten that the basic law of children's creativity is that its value lies not in its results, not in the product of creation, but in the process itself. It is not important what children create, but that they do create, that they exercise and implement their creative imagination.

(Vygotsky, in Holzman 2013)

Children's play is most likely to be creative when it is self-directed. Children can develop their imagination through role play, story-telling, or the expressive arts, when they can try out different ideas, work at their own pace and repeat ideas or move on when they are ready. Boys often choose to spend their time in self-directed play (Cigman 2014), outside or with open-ended materials such as blocks, sand or water. Carefully resourced indoor and outdoor provision enables boys' active, self-directed style of play to be channelled into creative expression.

Dylan is making a party hat. He divides a long strip of card into sections by measuring the sections with his hand span. He sticks identical pieces of paper onto each section, paper that he has cut to create a symmetrical 'snowflake' pattern. He stops and looks at his evolving creation, and he wraps the card into a cone shape. He holds it up in the air and says: *Who wants some of my ice cream?*

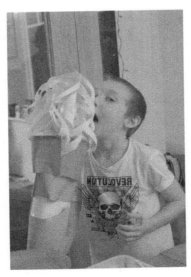

Children can:

- use their imagination to create whatever they want to create with open-ended materials that allow for chance discoveries, as we see with Dylan's creation that started as a hat and became an ice cream!

- discover how they can represent an image, a thought or an idea artistically, when they draw, paint and create models with a variety of two-dimensional and three-dimensional materials;

- explore colour, pattern and texture when they mix coloured paint and water and experiment with absorbent and non-absorbent surfaces;

- build up their fine motor dexterity by making large creations outside and small creations inside and outside;

- learn about pitch, tempo and rhythm in music when they make their own instruments from recycled materials and respond to music through dance and movement;

- explore different ways of being through storytelling, role play and small world play;

- make choices about which materials and tools they want to use to express themselves.

Resources in the continuous provision

- Natural materials, such as wool, string, shells, feathers, leaves, bark, and man-made materials, such as buttons and sequins that can be used for making collages and weaving on fences, in trees and in bushes, on garden netting;

- materials for 'transient' art: sand, mud, twigs, grasses, pebbles, spray bottles and washing-up liquid bottles filled with paint or coloured water, large brushes and rollers;

- long rolls of paper on the ground or on the wall, on or under tables;

- absorbent and non-absorbent paper and card: filter paper, blotting paper, paper with a gloss finish, sugar paper, thick and thin card;

- scissors, hole punches, staplers, thick and thin string and wool, duct tape and masking tape, different size brushes, pipettes;

- chalks and paints in mobile containers such as crates, buckets, lunch boxes and toolboxes;

- clay, gloop and play dough.

Children use pavement chalks as magic markers, map makers and to draw train tracks. They make a 'Cr wsh' ('car wash') with 'a drying bay' and a road

---

layout one day, and they make a dungeon another day. The chalk becomes a 'special button that will make your hand better' and it is used to keep score for a football game.

- Small loose parts that include: recycled materials; natural materials: cones, leaves, pebbles, sand, shells, moss, soil straws, wool, ribbons, bubble wrap, string; tubes and boxes in a range of sizes from tiny to huge; takeaway coffee cups (they make great wrist bands); wrapping paper, tissue paper, tin foil, material scraps; freezer bag fasteners, butterfly clips, pegs, glue, duct tape, masking tape, buttons.

A shoe box becomes a bed for Spiderman one day and a home for the guinea pig another day.

- Large loose parts that include: cardboard boxes; tyres, planks and crates; drainpipes and guttering;
- large hollow wooden blocks;
- dressing-up clothes, hats, masks, shoes, watches and jewellery for specific roles and for 'whatever you want to be . . .'.

Barney and Zachary take turns playing with the cape in the dressing-up corner. When Barney wears the cape, he becomes Batman. When Zachary wears the cape, he is Spiderman.

Places and spaces

- *Make a 'music den' outside with conventional musical instruments and recycled materials for children to make their own instruments.*
- *Create a performance area with microphones, music, ribbons and lightweight fabric, chairs in a circle, paper and card to make tickets and posters.*
- *Set up a small-scale model-making area inside and a large-scale model-making area outside.*
- *Create areas where children can explore media and materials on a small scale, in bowls and trays, and on a large scale on the floor and walls.*
- *Set up a 'whatever you want it to be' role-play area* (see Chapter 6).

(continued)

(continued)

- *Create magical spaces inside and outside*: a pop-up tent inside, and outside areas that change with the seasons. Provide different lighting – hand and head torches, colour filters – and create spaces that can only be reached through a tunnel or through bushes.

Challenge: Create a musical accompaniment for a favourite story. Make your own instruments from recycled materials that have loud and soft sounds, that you can shake, clash, bang, tap or blow into to make sounds.

5 Young writers and poets

Jack: *Are you proud of what I writ? I'm going to stick a jewel on, because I want to make the jewel all lovely.*

In general, boys take longer than girls to develop formal writing skills in the Early Years. However, they can become confident and skilful writers when they discover that writing is a valuable way of communicating, and when they see a purpose for their writing in their play (Cigman 2014).

Children can:

- develop their unique 'writer's voice' when they act out a superhero narrative in their play, and when they record their ideas by mark-making or orally, by talking into a voice or video recorder;

- develop compositional skills of writing when they draw and write about things that interest them;

- learn that marks on a page can carry meaning when they go on a treasure hunt;
- link spoken and written language when an adult scribes their stories and reads their words back to them;
- grow in confidence as writers, when they see their mark-making and writing displayed on the wall, in an author's area or as part of their play;
- improve their transcriptional skills (handwriting and phonic knowledge), when they write a platform sign for their role-play railway station or a letter to the dragon that left her egg in the garden: applying and practising their skills in their play.

Resources in the continuous provision

- Puppets, puppet theatres, masks;
- story stones, story sacks and storyboards;
- small world;
- 'writing on the move' bags, toolboxes, belts and lunch boxes with an inviting variety of writing resources;
- a writing trolley outside;
- inviting writing resources in boxes, everywhere, inside and outside;
- clipboards of different sizes;
- large rolls of paper on the floor and walls;
- large and small whiteboards and chalkboards, inside and outside;
- book boxes with fiction and non-fiction books.

Places and spaces

- *Create a book den* with fiction, poetry and non-fiction books, and books with strong rhythmic and rhyming language.
- *Create mark-making and writing stations and dens.*
- *Create a storytelling den* with a story chair and a story cape, and prompts for starting a story. Scribe children's stories or they can record a story onto a voice recorder or video recorder, or write themselves.
- *Create an author's area* with book-making resources, and a stand to display children's home-made books.

(continued)

(continued)

Children can fill bags with writing resources from the writing station to use in their play

- *Display environmental print* that has a purpose for children, and they can engage with: signs and labels, self-registration, ground rules for outside learning, and so on.
- *Display print from different languages.*

Large floor drawing indoors worked well. We gathered small groups of co-creators and shared storylines developed. There was lots of superhero/treasure finding stories from boys, negotiating and developing storylines. Kyle found this a great outlet for all his fast-paced verbal stories, which he often created whilst model-making in the creative workshop area. Adults enjoyed these experiences also, feeling it gave real opportunities for interactions with children.

(Reception teacher)

Challenge: Can you write a spell that will put a scary dragon to sleep?

Conclusion

Patrick is climbing a tree, taking his time, testing out his handholds and footholds until he feels secure to climb a little higher. A video camera strapped to his chest captures footage of his adventure from his perspective. It shows how he adjusts his balance and centre of gravity before he moves on and, when he turns and calls out in triumph, the camera captures the expression of Tim, the practitioner, who shares Patrick's delight.

The aim of this book has been to explore how we can develop our understanding of sex differences to support boys' learning 'without turning this knowledge into self-fulfilling prophecies' (Eliot 2012: 313). We know that children are gender detectives, picking up and learning ways of being from adults, other children and images around them. It is important that we let boys and girls express differences without allowing gender stereotypes to limit children's learning opportunities.

Children come into Early Years settings eager to continue the learning that began before birth. It is the privilege, but also the responsibility, of Early Years practitioners to create an environment that inspires, enthuses and engages all children. This book has shared ways to create an environment in response to our knowledge of young boys, an environment where boys can get 'up and running' in their learning and where girls will thrive equally.

We can't change the overall physical nature of the environment: some settings will have small tarmac outside areas, other settings will have acres of woodland. But we can use the space we have to the best effect. The aim of this book has been to offer some inspiring and manageable ways to extend the way we use the learning environment that we have, so that all children can learn without limits.

References and further reading

Athey, C. (2007) *Extending thought in young children: a parent-teacher partnership*. London: Paul Chapman Publishing.

Balbernie, R. (2011) *Circuits and circumstances: the consequences of early relationships – a viewpoint from interpersonal neurobiology*. Unicef UK Baby Friendly Initiative Annual Conference. Available at: http://unicef.org.uk/Documents/Baby_Friendly/Conference/Presentations/Robin_Balbernie_Baby_Friendly_Conference_2011.pdf (accessed 1 July 2016).

Bandura, A. (1977) *Social learning theory*. Englewood Cliffs, NJ: Prentice Hall.

Baron-Cohen, S. (2004) *The essential difference: men, women and the extreme male brain*. London: Penguin UK.

Bertram, A.D. (1996) *Effective early childhood educators: developing a methodology for improvement: Volume 1*. Unpublished PhD thesis. Coventry University.

Biddulph, S. (2003) *Raising boys: why boys are different – and how to help them become happy and balanced men*. London: Harper Thorson.

Blincoe, K. (2015) *Risk is essential to childhood – as are scrapes, grazes, falls and panic*. Available at: http://www.theguardian.com/commentisfree/2015/oct/14/risk-essential-childhood-children-danger (accessed 1 July 2016).

Broadhead, P., Howard, J. and Wood, E.A. (eds) (2010) *Play and learning in the early years*. London: Sage Publications Ltd.

Bruner, J. (1966) *Jerome Bruner and the process of education*. Available at: http://infed.org/mobi/jerome-bruner-and-the-process-of-education/ (accessed 1 July 2016).

Carr, S. (2001) *The boys are back in town*. London: Arrow Books.

Cigman, J. (2011) *Oxfordshire Boys' Writing Project report*. Available at: https://www.oxfordshire.gov.uk/cms/sites/default/files/folders/documents/childreneducationandfamilies/informationfor-childcareproviders/OxfordshireBoysWritingProjectReport.pdf (accessed 1 July 2016).

Cigman, J. (2014) *Supporting boys' writing in the early years: becoming a writer in leaps and bounds*. (David Fulton Books.) Abingdon: Routledge.

Clark, A. and Moss, P. (2011) *Listening to young children: the mosaic approach*. London: NCB.

Claxton, G. (2008) *What's the point of school?* Oxford: Oneworld.

Conversation, The (2016) Parents can help, but children take a DIY approach to learning language. *The Conversation*. 17 January. Available at: https://theconversation.com/parents-can-help-but-children-take-a-diy-approach-to-learning-language-53035 (accessed 25 August 2016).

DCSF (2007) *Confident, capable and creative: supporting boys' achievements*. Crown copyright.

DeBenedet, A.T. and Cohen Lawrence, J. (2011) *The art of roughhousing.* Philadelphia: Quirk Books.

Dewey, J. (1916) *Democracy and education: an introduction to the philosophy of education* (1966 edn). New York: Free Press.

DfE (2014a) *Statutory framework for the early years foundation stage.* Available at: https://www.gov.uk/government/uploads/system/uploads/attachment_data/file/335504/EYFS_framework_from_1_September_2014__with_clarification_note.pdf (accessed 1 July 2016).

DfE (2014b) *Early years foundation stage profile attainment by pupil characteristics, England 2014.* Available at: https://www.gov.uk/government/uploads/system/uploads/attachment_data/file/376216/SFR46_2014_text.pdf (accessed 1 July 2016).

Directorate for Education and Skills, OECD (2004) *Starting strong: curricula and pedagogies in early childhood education and care.* Available at: https://www.oecd.org/edu/school/31672150.pdf (accessed 26 August 2016).

Dowling, M. (2005) *Supporting children's sustained shared thinking.* London: British Association for Early Childhood Education.

Dowling, M. (2014) *Children under three years: the time of their lives.* London: Early Education. Available at: www.early-education.org.uk/children-under-three-years-time-their-lives (accessed 1 July 2016).

Dweck, C. (2012) *Mindset: how you can fulfil your potential.* New York: Ballantine Books.

Early Education (2012) *Development matters in the early years foundation stage.* Crown copyright.

Edwards, C., Gandini, L. and Formand, G. (eds) (2011) *The hundred languages of children: the Reggio Emilia experience in transformation.* Santa Barbara, CA: Praeger.

Eliot, L. (2011) *The myth of pink and blue brains.* Available at: http://www.ascd.org/publications/educational-leadership/summer11/vol68/num10/The-Myth-of-Pink-and-Blue-Brains.aspx (accessed 1 July 2016).

Eliot, L. (2012) *Pink brain, blue brain: how small differences grow into troublesome gaps – and what we can do about it.* Oxford: Oneworld.

Fine, C. (2011) *Delusions of gender.* London: Icon Books.

Fisher, J. (2016) *Interacting or interfering? Improving interactions in the early years.* Maidenhead: Open University Press.

Goddard Blythe, S. (2011) Physical foundations for learning. In House, R. (ed.) *Too Much, too soon? Early learning and the erosion of childhood* (pp. 131–46). Stroud: Hawthorn Press.

Gopnik, A. (2009) *The philosophical baby.* London: The Bodley Head.

Gopnik, A.M., Meltzoff, A.N. and Kuhl, P.K. (2007) *The scientist in the crib.* New York: HarperPerennial.

Gussin Paley, V. (1984) *Boys and girls: superheroes in the doll corner.* Chicago, IL: University of Chicago Press.

Gussin Paley, V. (1991) *The boy who would be a helicopter.* Boston, MA: Harvard University Press.

Holman, C. (2016) www.playfulfactory.com (accessed 1 July 2016).

Holzman, L. (2013) *Vygotsky: we're all unknown inventors.* Available at: http://loisholzman.org/2013/08/vygotsky-weall-all-unknown-inventors/ (accessed 1 July 2016).

Horizon (2014) Is your brain male or female? BBC2. 29 September.

Jarvis, P. (2010) 'Born to play': the biocultural roots of rough and tumble play, and its impact upon young children's learning. In Broadhead, P., Howard, J. and Wood E.A. (eds) *Play and learning in the early years* (pp. 61–77). London: Sage Publications Ltd.

Katz, L. (2015) *Lively minds: distinctions between academic versus intellectual goals for young children.* Available at: https://deyproject.files.wordpress.com/2015/04/dey-lively-minds-4-8-15.pdf (accessed 1 July 2016).

Laevers, F. (Ed.) (2005) *Sics (Ziko) wellbeing and involvement in care: a process-oriented self-evaluation instrument for care settings.* Kind & Gezin and Research Centre for Experiential Education.

Lowry, L. (2010) *Fact or fiction? The top 10 assumptions about early speech and language development.* Available at: http://www.hanen.org/helpful-info/articles/fact-or-fiction—the-top-10-assumptions-about-earl.aspx (accessed 25 August 2016).

MacLure, M. and Jones, L. (2009) *Classroom behaviour: why it's hard to be good.* Available at: http://www.esrc.ac.uk/news-and-events/press-releases/2821/Classroom_behaviour_why_its_hard_to_be_good.aspx (accessed 7 August 2013).

MacNaughton, G. and Williams, G. (2010) *Techniques for teaching young children: choices for theory and practice.* Maidenhead: Open University Press.

Malloch, S. and Trevarthen, C. (eds) (2009) *Communicative musicality: exploring the basis of human companionship.* Oxford: Oxford University Press.

Morton, K. (2015) Hundreds of under-fives excluded for disruptive behaviour. *Nursery World.* 30 July.

Moss, P. (2005) It's your choice. *Nursery World.* 24 November.

Moss, P. (2016) *The hundred languages of children know no age bounds.* Available at: https://ioelondonblog.wordpress.com/2016/03/23/the-hundred-languages-of-childhood-know-no-age-bounds/ (accessed 23 May 2016).

Moss, S. (2012) *Natural childhood.* National Trust. Available at: https://www.nationaltrust.org.uk/documents/read-our-natural-childhood-report.pdf (accessed 1 July 2016).

Moyles, J. (1989) *Just playing? Role and status of play in early childhood education.* Buckingham: Open University Press.

National Literacy Trust (2012) A third of dads are never seen reading. *Literacy News.* Available at: http://www.literacytrust.org.uk/news/5127_a_third_of_dads_are_never_seen_reading (accessed 1 July 2016).

Ofsted (2015) *Teaching and play in the early years – a balancing act?* https://www.gov.uk/government/publications/teaching-and-play-in-the-early-years-a-balancing-act (accessed 5 October 2016).

Panksepp, J. (2004) *Affective neuroscience: the foundations of human and animal emotions.* Oxford: Oxford University Press.

Piaget, J. (1957) *Construction of reality in the child.* London: Routledge & Kegan Paul.

Roberts, R. (2014) *Growing companionable wellbeing.* Early Education Conference. 14 May. Available at: https://early-education.org.uk/sites/default/files/growing_companionable_wellbeing.pdf (accessed 1 July 2016).

Rose, J. and Rogers, S. (2012) *The role of the adult in early years settings.* Maidenhead: Open University Press.

Smith, F. (1988) *Joining the literacy club.* Portsmouth, NH: Heinemann Educational.

Smith, M.K. (2002) Jerome S. Bruner and the process of education. *The Encyclopedia of Informal Education.* Available at: http://infed.org/mobi/jerome-bruner-and-the-process-of-education/ (accessed 1 July 2016).

Solly, K. (2015) *Risk, challenge and adventure in the early years.* (David Fulton Books.) Abingdon: Routledge.

Stewart, N. (2011) *How children learn: the characteristics of effective learning.* London: British Association for Early Childhood Education.

Strauss, V. (2015) How schools ruined recess – and four things needed to fix it. *Washington Post.* 4 February. Available at: https://www.washingtonpost.com/news/answer-sheet/wp/2015/02/04/how-schools-ruined-recess-and-four-things-needed-to-fix-it/ (accessed 24 August 2016).

Sylva, K., Melhuish, E.C., Sammons, P., Siraj-Blatchford, I. and Taggart, B. (2004) *Technical Paper 12: The final report: effective pre-school education.* London: Institute of Education, University of London.

Tizard, B. and Hughes, M. (1984) *Young children learning: talking and thinking at home and at school.* Waukegan, IL: Fontana Press.

Tovey, H. (2010) Playing on the edge: perceptions of risk and danger in outdoor play. In Broadhead, P., Howard, J. and Wood, E.A. (eds) *Play and learning in the early years* (pp. 79–94). London: Sage Publications Ltd.

Trevarthen, C. (2013) *Artful learning makes sense.* London: Early Education.

Vygotsky, L.S. (1978) *Mind in society: the development of higher psychological processes.* Cambridge, MA: Harvard University Press.

Vygotsky, L.S. (1987) Thinking and speech. In Rieber, R.W. and Carton, A.S. (eds) *The collected works of L.S. Vygotsky, Volume 1: Problems of general psychology* (pp. 39–285). New York: Plenum Press. (Original work published 1934.)

Wagner, E. (2014) David Mitchell, the master builder. *New Statesman.* Available at: http://www.newstatesman.com/culture/2014/10/david-mitchell-master-builder (accessed 1 July 2016).

Waller, T., Sandseter, E.B.H., Wyver, S., Arlemalm-Hagser, E. and Maynard, T. (2010) The dynamics of early childhood spaces: opportunities for outdoor play? *European Early Childhood Education Research Journal*, 18(4), pp. 437–43.

Wave Trust / DfE (2013) *Conception to age 2: the age of opportunity.* Available at: http://www.wavetrust.org/sites/default/files/reports/conception-to-age-2-full-report_0.pdf (accessed 1 July 2016).

Whitebread, D. (2010) Play, metacognition and self-regulation. In Broadhead, P., Howard, J. and Wood, E.A. (eds) *Play and learning in the early years* (pp. 161–76). London: Sage Publications Ltd.

Whitehead, M. (1997) *Language and literacy in the early years.* London: Sage Publications Ltd.

Index

Athey, C. 108

Balbernie, R. 9
Bandura, A. 9, 42; *see also* social learning theory
behaviour, and language 21, 40, 59
Biddulph, S. 38
boundaries: behavioural 37; personal 35, 74; physical 65
boundaries and expectations 3, 31, 38, 39, 41, 43, 57, 64, 69
boys' underachievement 1
Broadhead, P. 93, 94
Bruner, J. 113, 115; *see also* spiral curriculum

Carr, S. 35, 69
characteristics of effective learning 14, 37, 50
Cigman, J. 33, 38, 46, 48, 74, 85, 123, 126
Claxton, G. 9
code of behaviour 41, 42
cognitive development 63, 64, 77
companionable learning 37
construction 56, 64, 84, 90, 116, 118
Craft, A. 99; *see also* possibility thinking
creativity 57, 109, 122
curriculum in the Early Years 32, 50, 74, 77, 83, 101, 102, 112; *see also* creativity; literacy; maths; music; poetry; science; writing

dens 73, 90, 102, 109, 118, 127
development, holistic 32, 60
Dweck, C. 10–12, 33, 34

Early Years Foundation Stage (EYFS) 31, 34, 83; *see also* prime areas of learning; specific areas of learning
ECERS-R 65
Eliot, L. 7, 18, 19, 20, 21, 23, 24, 25, 33, 56, 59, 64, 69, 76, 80, 83, 84, 85, 118, 129
emotional development 37, 51, 97, 107
EPPE research 32
executive function 13, 14
expectations, for children as learners 10, 26, 29, 33, 64, 65, 76
expectations, parental 19, 28, 76

Fine, C. 19
Fisher, J. 85

gender detectives 18–19, 129
gender differences: and environment 18, 22, 24, 29; and brain development 7, 8, 18, 21, 80; and empathetic skills 21; and hormones 21; and inhibitory control 21, 34; and language development 80, 83–5, 95; and visual spatial skills 21, 25
gender gap, and language 80, 83–5
gender identity 17, 18, 22
gender-specific play 18, 24, 56, 84
gender stereotypes, challenging 22, 25, 26, 27, 28, 43, 62
Goddard Blythe, S. 63
Gopnik, A. 14, 34
Gussin Paley, V. 85, 90

home learning environment 32, 95

imaginative companionship 81
inner speech 82

Katz, L. 32, 33, 50, 51, 54, 67

Laevers, F. 46, 53, 60, 62, 63
language: and communication skills 51, 64,
    77, 102, 103; and culture 81; and feelings
    43, 51, 82; and learning 81–2, 93, 102;
    playing with 88; and relationships 24, 81,
    82; of thinking 59
language skills, acquiring 79–80, 81, 82,
    83, 85
learning: academic 32, 51; active 43; deep
    level 46, 53; holistic 32, 60, 63; intellectual
    32
learning dispositions 9, 13, 15, 28, 32, 50, 58,
    63, 102
learning environment, inclusive 43, 56
learning styles 43, 48
literacy 102, 103, 104, 105, 107
loose parts 57, 65, 70, 71, 72, 73, 77, 90,
    118, 125

MacMillan, M. 34
Malaguzzi, L. 1, 3, 98, 99
management issues 74
maths 102, 103, 104, 116
mindsets for learning 10–12
Mitchell, D. 115
Moss, P. 1, 3, 36, 98, 99
motivation, intrinsic 10, 46, 52, 53, 62, 99
motor skills: 63, 64, 69, 70, 71, 73; fine 20,
    31, 33, 39, 51, 52, 57, 58, 62, 63; gross
    24, 34, 64
mud kitchen 70, 72, 73, 104, 106, 107, 122
music 122, 124, 125, 126

neurosexism 19

observational assessment 15, 108
OECD 62
Ofsted 2, 99

parents: attitudes to gender 28, 56;
    communication with 28, 38, 40, 43,
    52, 54, 76–7, 95, 111–12, 119
physical development 51, 97, 107
Piaget, J. 81, 98
planning: the environment 65, 100; for
    predictable interests 102; in the moment
    69, 100, 101, 102; for routines 107
plasticity, of the brain 8, 9, 18, 21, 29
play: physical 63, 64, 71, 76, 77; rough and
    tumble 42, 52, 65, 68, 69, 90, 109; see
    also rough housing
play and exploration 4, 83
poetry 127
possibility thinking 99
predictable interests 53, 73, 74, 102, 108
prime areas of learning 97; see also Early
    Years Foundation Stage
private speech 40, 81, 82
provocations for learning 51, 53

Reggio Emilia 74, 98
resources, inclusive 56
risk: reduction 35; benefits 57, 77; benefit
    assessments 36; management 38
Roberts, R. 37
role models 8, 10, 26, 42, 51, 76, 115
role play 14, 76, 84, 90, 91, 94, 104–6, 118,
    122–5, 127
rough housing 68, 69, 76; see also rough
    and tumble
routines 40, 59, 88, 107

schema 108–9, 113
science 39, 102, 103, 104, 107, 116
self-efficacy 9–10, 12, 15
self-regulation 4, 12–14, 15, 58, 85–6, 89,
    103
social constructivism 3, 98
social development 34, 95
social learning theory 42
social play continuum 92
social referencing 8–9, 15, 25, 40
specific areas of learning 98; see also Early
    Years Foundation Stage

spiral curriculum 116
stereotype threat 33, 43
Stewart, N. 8, 9, 40, 100
sustained shared thinking 86–7
Sylva, K. 32, 65, 86, 95

tinkering workshop 52–3, 55, 56–8, 60
Tizard, B., and Hughes, M. 84, 98
Tovey, H. 38, 74
Trevarthen, C. 8, 80, 81
transitions 40, 59

vestibular system 41
Vygotsky, L. 4, 5, 40, 81, 82, 98, 122

wellbeing and involvement levels 46–8, 53,
    60, 62–3, 102
'whatever you want it to be' place 93–4, 125
Whitehead, M. 81, 82, 88, 95
writing 20, 33, 54, 64, 95, 102, 104, 107,
    110, 121, 126, 127, 128

zone of proximal development 4

Taylor & Francis eBooks

Helping you to choose the right eBooks for your Library

Add Routledge titles to your library's digital collection today. Taylor and Francis ebooks contains over 50,000 titles in the Humanities, Social Sciences, Behavioural Sciences, Built Environment and Law.

Choose from a range of subject packages or create your own!

Benefits for you
» Free MARC records
» COUNTER-compliant usage statistics
» Flexible purchase and pricing options
» All titles DRM-free.

Benefits for your user
» Off-site, anytime access via Athens or referring URL
» Print or copy pages or chapters
» Full content search
» Bookmark, highlight and annotate text
» Access to thousands of pages of quality research at the click of a button.

REQUEST YOUR FREE INSTITUTIONAL TRIAL TODAY

Free Trials Available
We offer free trials to qualifying academic, corporate and government customers.

eCollections – Choose from over 30 subject eCollections, including:

Archaeology	Language Learning
Architecture	Law
Asian Studies	Literature
Business & Management	Media & Communication
Classical Studies	Middle East Studies
Construction	Music
Creative & Media Arts	Philosophy
Criminology & Criminal Justice	Planning
Economics	Politics
Education	Psychology & Mental Health
Energy	Religion
Engineering	Security
English Language & Linguistics	Social Work
Environment & Sustainability	Sociology
Geography	Sport
Health Studies	Theatre & Performance
History	Tourism, Hospitality & Events

For more information, pricing enquiries or to order a free trial, please contact your local sales team:
www.tandfebooks.com/page/sales

 Routledge
Taylor & Francis Group

The home of
Routledge books

www.tandfebooks.com